I0820297

BAKE IT OFF

BAKE IT OFF

TASTY TAYLOR SWIFT-INSPIRED BAKES

UNOFFICIAL & UNAUTHORISED

Elly McCausland

Photography by Ellis Parrinder

CONTENTS

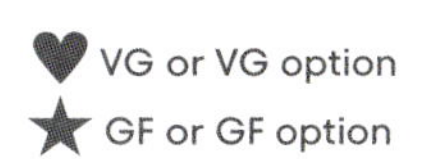

♥ VG or VG option
★ GF or GF option

INTRODUCTION

Dear Reader,

Welcome to *Bake It Off*. It's been waiting for you...

This is the ultimate collection of baking recipes inspired by the world of Taylor Swift. Because the devil's in the detail, the recipes in this book take inspiration from the entire Taylor Swift universe: lyrics, eras, Easter eggs and aesthetics. Whether you're a fearless baking pro, a lover of learning or making your debut in the world of cake and cookies, there's something here for anyone looking to enhance their culinary reputation.

You'll find recipes inspired by all 11 of Taylor's eras – from a bundt cake that tells a love story to a bittersweet dessert fit for a Tortured Poet. Most are simple and easy to follow, with a few more elaborate creations for when you're really looking to show off and make the whole place shimmer. You'll find sweet and savoury tarts and pies, delicious cakes and cookies, breads and brownies, and everything in between. There are also vegan and gluten-free options throughout and flavours from across the globe.

Whip up creations out of your wildest dreams, or cosy up with timeless classics as the leaves turn and the air gets colder and colder. If you like shiny things, you're in for a treat – there's edible glitter aplenty in these bejeweled bakes, and all the colours of the rainbow, from key lime green to burning red.

It's nice to have a friend, so at the back of the book you'll find menu suggestions for themed gatherings – from baby showers to book club meetings. But if you want to draw the curtains closed and eat your creations all alone, I won't judge.

Are you ready for it?

Elly x

THE ERAS

Debut

FEARLESS

Speak Now

RED

1989

Reputation

Lover

folklore

evermore

Midnights

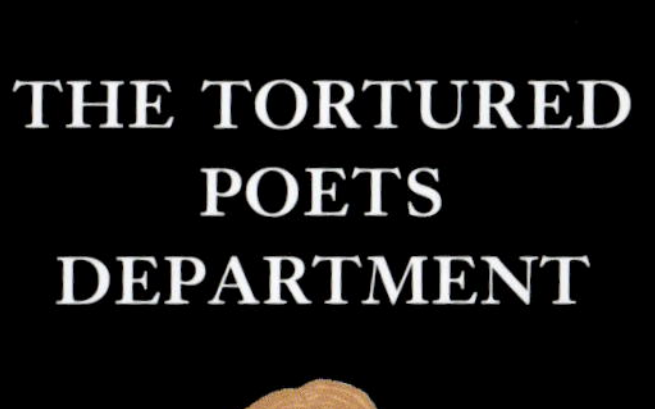

Debut

A box of unread letters under a bed. A tear-stained guitar. The slam of a screen door. Little black dresses, faded blue jeans and pickup trucks. Moonlight on the lake and roses in the hallway. Trying to find a place in this world, but feeling invisible on the outside.

Welcome to your baking Debut. This is an era of creature comforts, of wholesome country classics that have stayed beautiful throughout the ages. Even if you feel like you're coming undone, there's always joy to be had in baking from your perfectly good heart. Bring the magic of Georgia stars into the kitchen with a summery cobbler that'll make you think happiness, or chill with a delightful citrus cheesecake that's only the good kind of cold. Put that picture down and get some sleep tonight, then treat yourself to a platter of juicy drop scones in the morning. Or go back to the days of young love, of sneaking out late and tapping on windows, with a timeless apple pie – oh my my my.

If these recipes were a song, you'd be wanting to play it again and again.

(tear) Drop scones

Drop scones are a British name for fluffy, round pancakes. These couldn't be easier to make and are perfect for breakfast or brunch, coming together in minutes, though they do benefit from a brief rest before cooking. I've added a scattering of blueberries in homage to those famous teardrops that launched a career. You can make the batter in advance and leave it in the fridge overnight, ready for the morning – wake up to a treat that will feel like a wish from a wishing star.

SERVES 2–3

175g self-raising flour
1 tsp baking powder
Zest of 1 lemon
50g caster sugar
1 egg
1 tsp vanilla extract
200ml whole or semi-skimmed milk
45g butter, plus extra to serve
175g fresh or frozen blueberries
Icing sugar, for dusting
Maple syrup, to serve

1. Sift the flour into a medium bowl, then whisk in the baking powder, lemon zest and sugar. Make a well in the centre, then add the egg, vanilla and milk. Whisk from the centre outwards, gradually incorporating more of the flour until you have a smooth, lump-free batter. If you have time, leave the batter to rest for 30–60 minutes (this helps to relax the gluten, making fluffier pancakes).
2. Melt the butter in a large, non-stick frying pan over a medium-high heat. Using a ladle, tip dollops of batter into the pan, so they spread out to make pancakes around 10cm (4in) in diameter. Leave at least 2.5cm (1in) of space between each pancake. You may need to do this in batches depending on the size of your pan. Sprinkle 1 tablespoon of the blueberries over each dollop of batter.
3. Once bubbles start to appear, flip the pancakes over using a spatula or palette knife. Cook for another 1–2 minutes on the other side. Remove to a plate and keep warm in a low oven while you cook the remaining pancakes. Repeat until all the batter and blueberries are used up.
4. Serve warm, dusted with icing sugar and with maple syrup for drizzling over. Add a knob of butter before serving for extra luxury.

Georgia stars peach cobbler

Even when you've woken up to find summer gone, you can revisit it with this dish of sunshine. I debated calling this recipe 'Thyme McGraw', but the pun seemed just too awful. The inclusion of lemon thyme in this cobbler is not, however: it adds a freshness to the sweet peaches, which – along with the cornmeal – are the obvious choice for a recipe themed around Georgia. Use regular thyme if you can't find it, or rosemary or lavender. When you think happiness, I hope you think of this peach cobbler.

SERVES 8

Equipment: 25 x 35cm (10 x 14in) baking dish; star-shaped cookie cutter

♥ VG: use plant-based butter and buttermilk alternatives

85g cold butter, cut into cubes, plus extra for greasing
1kg ripe peaches
65g light brown sugar
Zest of 1 lemon, plus 2 tbsp juice
1 tbsp cornflour
2 tsp fresh lemon thyme leaves
150g plain flour, plus extra for rolling
70g cornmeal
1½ tsp baking powder
½ tsp flaky salt
60g finely chopped pecan nuts
240ml buttermilk
2 tbsp demerara sugar
Vanilla ice cream, to serve

1 Preheat the oven to 170°C fan/190°C/375°F/gas 5. Grease the baking dish with butter.

2 Cut the peaches into slices around 1cm (½in) thick and discard the stones. Put the peaches in the baking dish with the brown sugar, lemon zest and juice, cornflour and thyme leaves, then toss well. Set aside.

3 In a large bowl, add the flour, cornmeal, baking powder, salt and butter. Rub the butter into the flour with your fingertips until the mixture resembles fine breadcrumbs (you can also do this in a food processor). Stir in the pecan nuts. Add the buttermilk to make a soft but not sticky dough – you may not need it all.

4 Place the dough on a lightly floured work surface and pat out with your hands to form a rectangle around 2.5cm (1in) thick. Use a star-shaped cookie cutter, or a sharp knife, to cut star shapes from the dough, then place them on top of the peach mixture, about 4cm (1½in) apart. Repeat until all the dough is used up.

5 Sprinkle the stars with the demerara sugar. Bake for 30–40 minutes, until the peaches are bubbling and the topping is golden brown. Leave to cool for 15 minutes before serving with vanilla ice cream.

Cold as yuzu cheesecake

Next time you want to start a fight because you need to feel something, make this cheesecake instead. The sharp, aromatic tang of yuzu, a Japanese citrus fruit, will give you chills – but the good kind. (You can buy bottled yuzu juice at Asian supermarkets and online, and you might find the fresh fruit in specialist shops during winter. If you can't find it, limes or lemons make good substitutes.) This cake makes a perfect end to a perfect day, or a dinner party – you can make it in advance and let it set, so you just take it out of the fridge when you're ready to serve. There'll be no fake smiles once your guests dive in.

SERVES 6–8

Equipment: 20cm (8in) springform round cake tin, food processor

★ GF: use gluten-free biscuits in the base

110g butter, plus extra for greasing
200g digestive biscuits
300g plain quark or ricotta cheese
200g full-fat cream cheese
150g icing sugar
Zest of 2 fresh yuzu, lemons or limes
4 gelatine sheets
4 tbsp fresh or bottled yuzu juice, or fresh lemon/lime juice

1 Preheat the oven to 180°C fan/200°C/400°F/gas 6. Grease the cake tin and line the base with a circle of baking parchment.

2 Blitz the biscuits in a food processor to fine crumbs. Melt the butter in a small saucepan, then add the biscuit crumbs. Stir well to combine. Tip onto the base of the cake tin and press down with the back of a spoon to form an even layer. Bake for 10 minutes, until golden. Leave to cool.

3 Whisk the quark or ricotta, cream cheese, icing sugar and yuzu (or lemon or lime) zest together in a large bowl. Soak the gelatine sheets for a couple of minutes in a jug of water, until soft and pliable.

4 Put the yuzu (or alternative citrus) juice in a small saucepan over a medium heat. Bring it almost to the boil (so it starts to steam), then turn off the heat. Squeeze the water out of the gelatine sheets, then add them to the juice. Stir briefly until the gelatine is completely dissolved.

5 Have your whisk ready, then pour the gelatine and juice mixture slowly into the cheese mixture, whisking constantly to incorporate. Pour over the biscuit base and place in the fridge for at least 6 hours to set.

(rose) Mary's song (oh pie pie pie)

You and pie – oh my my my. Whatever your age, few things are better than the magic combination of fruit and pastry. The herbal perfume of rosemary adds a lovely twist to this classic apple and blackberry pie – just the sort of homely thing you'd want to eat while sitting on your front porch, remembering when your world was one block wide. Your mama might roll her eyes, but you can share this pie with whoever you like. I hope you'll still be making it when you're 87 and 89.

Equipment: 23cm (9in) non-stick pie dish, food processor (optional)

★ GF: use shop-bought gluten-free pastry

For the pastry:
420g plain flour
270g cold butter, cut into cubes
6 tbsp caster sugar
A pinch of salt
3–5 tbsp ice-cold water

For the filling:
700g sharp cooking apples (such as Bramley's)
2 tsp lemon juice
1 tsp finely chopped fresh rosemary leaves
100g golden caster sugar
3 tbsp cornflour
100g fresh or frozen blackberries

To finish:
1 egg, beaten
Rosemary sprigs, to decorate (optional)
Icing sugar, for dusting (optional)

photographed overleaf

1 Make the pastry. Put the flour, butter, sugar and salt into a large bowl. Rub the butter into the mixture using your fingertips, until it resembles fine breadcrumbs. You can also do this in a food processor. Add the water, a little at a time, until the mixture starts to clump – you may not need it all. Bring it together to form a soft dough, then divide into two pieces and press each into a flat disc. Wrap each in cling film and chill for 30 minutes.

2 Meanwhile, make the filling. Peel and core the cooking apples, then cut into 1cm (½in) thick slices. Put in a bowl and toss with the remaining filling ingredients. Set aside. Preheat the oven to 180°C fan/200°C/400°F/gas 6.

3 Roll one of the pastry discs out to around 5mm (¼in) thick. Use it to line the pie dish. There will be some overhang, but leave it for now.

4 Pour the apple filling into the pastry-lined dish.

5 Roll the remaining disc of pastry out to around 5mm (¼in) thick. Drape it over the filled pie. Use a knife to trim around the edge of the pie dish, then crimp the edges together using a fork or your fingers. Use any remaining pastry to decorate the pie – for example, with the numbers '87' and '89'.

6 Brush the top of the pie with the beaten egg and decorate with rosemary sprigs, if you like. Cut two small slits in the middle of the pie to let out the steam while the pie is baking.

7 Bake for 15 minutes, then lower the heat to 160°C fan/180°C/350°F/gas 4 and bake for another 15–20 minutes, until the pie is deep gold.

8 Cool completely on a wire rack before dusting with icing sugar, if liked, and serving.

87

FEARLESS

Go dance in your best dress. Send a message in a bottle – or perhaps in a cake box. Baking is a love story, and you're about to just say 'yes'.

Feel perfectly fine as you jump then fall in love with a beautiful bundt, or throw together a bunch of rock cakes too good to toss at a beloved's window. You may not be a princess, but you can bake your way into a fairy tale for a little while. It's an era of golden skies and glowing pavements; of romance played out in the pouring rain. Bring all this into the kitchen with a luscious appetiser that belongs with you, whether you wear short skirts or T-shirts. Put childhood nostalgia on a plate with cupcakes that bring back those best days. Spread joy to those on the other side of your door, whether it's your Romeo or your little brother, your best friend or your mother.

Be fearless with flour, make fairy tales with your mixer and bake some memories that will last forever and always.

LOVE STORY CAKE

Just say 'yes' to this beauty of a bundt cake that you'll want to take somewhere you can be alone. It's inspired by the flavours Juliet might have enjoyed in fair Verona – sweet, Marsala-soaked raisins, olive oil and lemons. The décor is glitter and gold to evoke the lights, the parties and the ballgowns of yesteryear. Be sure to grease your tin really thoroughly to prevent the cake sticking. This is best enjoyed on a balcony in the balmy air of summer.

SERVES 10–12

Equipment: 2.4 litre (2.5 quart) bundt or kugelhopf tin (I recommend those by Nordic Ware); an electric stand mixer or electric hand whisk

For the cake:
120ml Marsala or other sweet Italian wine
90g raisins
Cake-release spray, or 2 tbsp soft margarine mixed with 2 tbsp vegetable oil and 1 tbsp plain flour
Zest and juice of 3 lemons
265g golden caster sugar
5 eggs
160ml light olive oil (an inexpensive one is fine)
280g self-raising flour

For the icing and decoration:
90g icing sugar
2–3 tsp lemon juice (reserved from the cake ingredients)
2 tsp edible liquid bronze or gold lustre
Chocolate hearts
Edible gold glitter or powdered lustre spray

1 Put the Marsala into a small saucepan and bring to the boil over a high heat, then lower the heat to a gentle simmer. Add the raisins and simmer for 5 minutes, stirring occasionally. Turn off the heat and leave for 15–20 minutes so that the raisins plump up.

2 Preheat the oven to 170°C fan/190°C/375°F/gas 3. Grease the bundt tin with cake release spray, or whisk together the margarine, vegetable oil and flour and use a piece of kitchen roll to smear it all over the inside of the tin, making sure you get into all the creases.

3 Put the lemon zest and caster sugar into the bowl of an electric stand mixer, or a large bowl. Rub the zest into the sugar using your fingertips to release the fragrant oils.

4 Add the eggs, then beat everything together on a high speed using the mixer or an electric whisk, for about 5 minutes, until the mixture looks thick and pale.

5 Juice the lemons and set aside 3 teaspoons of the juice. With the mixer or whisk running on a low speed, gradually add the olive oil and lemon juice (except the 3 teaspoons) until you have a smooth batter.

6 Sift the flour into the bowl and tip in the raisins and the soaking Marsala. Gently mix together until just combined.

7 Pour the mixture into the prepared tin and bake for 40 minutes, or until a skewer inserted into the middle comes out clean. Wait 10 minutes before turning the cake out of the tin onto a wire rack, then leave to cool completely.

continued overleaf

8 While the cake cools, make the icing. Put the icing sugar in a large bowl and gradually add the lemon juice, whisking, until you have a thick mixture. Add the liquid bronze or gold lustre, a few drops at a time, until you have a drizzle-able icing with a metallic sheen. Spoon this all over the cold cake, allowing it to generously run down the sides, leaving some cake visible.

9 While the icing is still wet, stick chocolate hearts to the side of the cake. Finally, spray with gold glitter or lustre to finish.

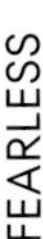

THROWIN' ROCK CAKES

There's an awful lot of rock- and pebble-throwing in *Fearless*. If you want something a little less dangerous to throw at your beloved's window, I recommend these rock cakes; or, better still, don't throw them at all – just eat them. Rock cakes are somewhere between a scone and a cookie; not too sweet, but delightfully crumbly. In the spirit of throwing pebbles, I've packed these with delicious stone fruits – dried apricots and prunes. They're irresistible fresh from the oven and topped with a little salted butter.

MAKES 12

230g self-raising flour
75g golden caster sugar
1 tsp baking powder
1 tsp ground cinnamon
120g cold butter, cut into cubes
60g chopped dried apricots
60g chopped dried prunes
1 egg, beaten
1 tsp vanilla extract
2 tbsp milk, plus extra for brushing
2 tbsp demerara sugar, for sprinkling

1. Preheat the oven to 160°C fan/180°C/350°F/gas 4. Line a baking tray with baking parchment or a non-stick liner.
2. Put the flour, caster sugar, baking powder and cinnamon into a large bowl and mix. Add the butter, then rub into the flour with your fingertips until the mixture resembles fine breadcrumbs (you can also do this in a food processor). Stir in the apricots and prunes.
3. Add the egg, vanilla and milk and use your hands to bring the mixture together into a soft dough. Don't overwork it.
4. Divide the mixture into balls and place on the baking tray, evenly spaced apart. Press down gently on each ball to flatten them slightly. Brush the top of each ball with a little milk, then sprinkle with the demerara sugar.
5. Bake for 25 minutes, until the cakes have risen a little and turned light golden. Leave to cool before eating.

YOU BELONG WITH BRIE

Is there a match more perfect than the girl on the bleachers and the boy whom only she understands? This recipe might be a serious contender. Few ingredients belong together more than fruit and cheese, and this melting baked Brie with a tangy fig jam centre is as gloriously satisfying as the final moments of the 'You Belong With Me' video. If you prefer, you can swap out the fig jam for blackcurrant. Serve as a very lazy appetiser: it only requires about two minutes of hands-on time, but all your guests will dive in once it's served up.

SERVES 4

Equipment: 2 small baking dishes – 1 to fit the cheese snugly

★ GF: serve with gluten-free crackers or bread

60g chopped walnuts
A whole Brie cheese (you can also use Camembert)
6 tbsp fig jam
2 tsp fresh thyme leaves or chopped fresh rosemary leaves
3 tsp runny honey
Crackers or good crusty bread, to serve

1 Preheat the oven to 180°C fan/200°C/400°F/gas 6.

2 Put the walnuts in a small baking dish and toast in the oven for 6–8 minutes, until slightly darker and fragrant. Set aside to cool.

3 Take a small baking dish, the right size to fit the wheel of Brie snugly, slice the Brie in half horizontally, then put one half in the dish, cut side up. Take half the walnuts and press them gently into the cut surface of the cheese. Dollop the fig jam onto the cheese and roughly spread it, leaving a border of about 2cm (¾in) around the edge. Sprinkle over half the thyme/rosemary.

4 Put the other piece of Brie on top, rind side facing up (essentially sandwiching the two halves together). Press the remaining walnuts into the top of the cheese. Drizzle over the honey and sprinkle with the remaining thyme/rosemary.

5 Bake for 20 minutes.

6 Remove from the oven, leave for 5 minutes, then dive in with gluten-free crackers or bread.

PUMPKIN PATCH CUPCAKES

Ready to have The Best Day? If the trees are starting to change in the fall and you're feeling the need to put your big coat on, it's a sign that it's the season to whip up a batch of these cupcakes. They are warm with pumpkin spice, topped with a delicious pumpkin frosting and crowned with adorable little fondant pumpkins – perfect for Halloween, Thanksgiving or just a cosy evening in.

MAKES 12

Equipment: 12-hole muffin tin with paper cases, an electric stand mixer or electric hand whisk, piping bag and nozzle (optional), cocktail stick

For the cupcakes:
150g plain flour
1 tsp baking powder
½ tsp bicarbonate of soda
140g dark brown sugar
½ tsp flaky salt
2 tsp mixed spice or pumpkin spice
100ml rapeseed oil
2 eggs
250g pumpkin purée
1 tsp vanilla extract

For the frosting:
110g soft butter
100g pumpkin purée
120g full-fat cream cheese
240g icing sugar
Zest of 1 orange

For the decorative pumpkins:
225g orange fondant icing
20g green fondant icing

1. Preheat the oven to 180°C fan/200°C/400°F/gas 6. Line the muffin tin with the paper cases.
2. Whisk together the flour, baking powder, bicarbonate of soda, brown sugar, salt and spice. In a separate bowl or jug, whisk together the oil, eggs, pumpkin purée and vanilla.
3. Gently mix the wet ingredients into the dry until just combined – don't overmix. Divide the mixture between each muffin case.
4. Bake for 20 minutes, until risen and golden. The tops should spring back when lightly pressed with a finger. Transfer to a wire rack and leave to cool completely.
5. Make the frosting by whisking everything together in a medium bowl, or stand mixer, until smooth and thick. Place in the fridge for 30 minutes to firm up.
6. Transfer the frosting to a piping bag and pipe it over each cupcake into a swirl (or dollop it on with a spoon if you're feeling lazy).
7. For the fondant pumpkins, divide your orange fondant into twelve equal-sized balls. Squash each ball very slightly with your palm on a flat surface. Use the side of a cocktail stick to create ridges around each ball like a pumpkin. Use the blunt end of the stick to make a little hole in the top of each pumpkin. Roll the green fondant into twelve small stalks and place one end of each in each hole. Top each frosted cupcake with a pumpkin.

Speak Now

Long live this collection of recipes. They're not mine, they're ours, and I think you'll be enchanted to meet them.

Make sparks fly with your mixer as you put a (Taylor's Version) twist on classics that never grow old. Watch your castles crumble in the best way, into a mass of succulent, bubbling fruit. Live in a chess game you'll actually enjoy, since it's flavoured with delicate violet petals and almonds and is certainly not going to mess with you (though it might mess up your dress). Crown your kitchen with sweet tangles of dough that will make the crowd go wild. It's an era of pastels and enchantment, fireflies and superheroes, dragon-fighting and lullaby-singing, all yours at the electric touch of a whisk. Shape your pastries like gowns, shine like fireworks and create a new timeless tradition that speaks for itself.

Do say 'yes – let's run away now'.

A pastry shaped like a gown - Chess game Battenberg cake
Long live blueberry and almond couronne - Castles crumble

A pastry shaped like a gown

Let your imagination run away now with some wild ideas for decorating these meringues. They're far cheaper than a wedding gown, and much tastier, with delicious fudgy insides and a crisp outer shell. Offer them round at tea time and everyone will speak now – asking for more! The recipe itself is simple, which means you can devote a little time to creating mini masterpieces with edible glitter and sprinkles. Dried berry powders are available online and are great for adding both colour and flavour.

MAKES AROUND 10

Equipment: electric stand mixer or electric hand whisk

★ GF: make sure your sprinkles and decorations are gluten-free

For the meringues:
6 egg whites
350g caster sugar

To decorate:
2 tbsp apricot jam
Sprinkles of your choice
4 tbsp freeze-dried strawberry or raspberries pieces (or both)
Edible lustre or glitter (pink, purple and silver work well), and/or dried raspberry or strawberry powder

1 Preheat the oven to 120°C fan/140°C/275°F/gas 1. Line two baking sheets with baking parchment or non-stick liners.

2 Place the egg whites in the bowl of an electric stand mixer fitted with a whisk attachment, or a large bowl. Make sure the bowl is completely clean and free of grease beforehand.

3 Using the stand mixer or an electric whisk, beat the egg whites at a high speed until they turn solid white and stand up in stiff peaks. Once they reach this stage, continue to whisk at speed, adding the sugar gradually until the whites are thick, glossy and stiff.

4 Using a large spoon, place about 10 dollops of the mixture onto the prepared baking trays. Use the spoon to smooth them into a spiral shape, upwards, so they're loosely cone-shaped.

5 Put the meringues in the oven and immediately lower the heat to 100°C fan/120°C/250°F/gas ½. Bake for 2 hours, then turn off the heat and leave the meringues to cool completely in the oven without opening the door – this ensures a fudgy centre and no cracks.

6 Once the meringues are cool, put the apricot jam in a small saucepan with 1 tablespoon of water and bring to the boil. Cook, stirring, for 1 minute until syrupy, then remove from the heat.

7 Brush the jam over the cooled meringues and use it to stick on your sprinkles and/or freeze-dried berry pieces. Finally, spritz with edible lustre or dust with edible glitter and/or dried berry powder.

Chess game Battenberg cake

I change the rules every day. A traditional Battenberg cake only has four squares, which are coloured pink and white. This one is pretty in Speak Now pastels and has more squares – closer, in fact, to the original, which was baked in England in 1884 to celebrate the wedding of Prince Louis of Battenberg and Princess Victoria (during which everyone held their peace and no one ran away). I've put a floral twist on it with violet petal jam, though you can use raspberry or apricot to be more traditional. It looks complicated, but it's actually easy to assemble.

SERVES 6–8

Equipment: two 20cm (8in) square cake tins, an electric stand mixer or electric hand whisk

For the cakes:
360g soft butter, plus extra for greasing
360g caster sugar
6 eggs, beaten
80g ground almonds
300g self-raising flour
1 tsp baking powder
½–1 tsp pink food colouring
½ tsp vanilla extract
½–1 tsp violet food colouring
½ tsp almond extract

To decorate:
4 tbsp violet petal jam, or raspberry or apricot jam
250g marzipan

1. Preheat the oven to 160°C fan/180°C/350°F/gas 4. Grease the cake tins and line with baking parchment.
2. Beat the butter and sugar using an electric whisk or stand mixer until light and fluffy – about 3–5 minutes. Gradually add the eggs, whisking well between each addition. If the mixture starts to curdle, add 1 tablespoon of the ground almonds. Once the eggs are whisked in, add the remaining ground almonds, the flour and baking powder and mix just enough to combine.
3. Weigh the mixture in the bowl. Transfer half of it to a clean bowl and add the pink food colouring (start with ½ teaspoon and add more if necessary) and vanilla, mixing briefly until you have a light pink batter. Pour this into one of the prepared tins.
4. To the remaining batter in the original bowl, add the violet food colouring (start with ½ teaspoon and add more as needed) and almond extract, mixing so that you have a bright violet batter. Pour this into the other cake tin.
5. Bake both cakes for 35 minutes, until they are risen, golden and spring back when lightly pressed in the centre. Don't be alarmed if the violet sponge looks green on top! Set aside to cool briefly in the tins, then transfer to a wire rack to cool completely.
6. To assemble, first measure how high each cooled cake is. If one is slightly lower than the other, use the lower measurement. Cut each cake into five strips the width of this measurement. For example, if your lowest cake is 3cm (1¼in) high, cut each square cake into five 3cm (1¼in) wide strips. There may be some cake left over.

continued overleaf

7 Put the jam into a small saucepan with 1 tablespoon water and heat gently, stirring, until it starts to bubble. Turn off the heat – you should have a syrupy glaze.

8 Roll out the marzipan as thinly as possible – around 3mm (⅛in) – to form a 40 x 30cm (16 x 12in) rectangle. Place it onto a sheet of baking parchment (this will make it easier to assemble the cake). Brush the marzipan all over with the jam glaze.

9 Trim all your strips of cake so they are 15cm (6in) long. Set the offcuts aside.

10 Place the marzipan (on the paper) in front of you with the long side facing you. Place a pink strip of cake in the middle, vertically. Brush the strip of cake all over with the jam glaze. Now place a strip of purple cake on either side. You want all three strips of cake to be exactly the same height, so trim off any higher bits using a knife held horizontally. Now brush them all over with the jam glaze.

11 Repeat the process but place pink strips of cake on top of the purple below, and vice versa (so purple in the middle, a pink on either side). Again, trim to make sure they're all the same height. Brush all over with the glaze. Repeat once more, again alternating the colours. Brush with the glaze.

12 Using the paper to help you lift it, wrap the shorter sides of the marzipan tightly around the cake. It should overlap slightly – use the paper to help you flip over the whole cake, so the overlap is underneath and hidden. Trim the remaining marzipan from the square edges of the cake so you can see the chequerboard pattern of the cake inside.

13 Chill the cake, still wrapped in its paper, for an hour before slicing.

Long live blueberry and almond couronne

You'd definitely swap your baseball cap for this crown. A couronne – 'crown' in French – is a traditional French bread often served at Christmas. My version is scented with cardamom and packed full of flavoursome berries and marzipan. It's gooey, chewy and delicious, and simpler to make than you would think from looking at it – much easier than slaying a dragon – but it does require some advance planning. A thin sliver is delicious for afternoon tea, or serve a bigger portion with some fresh berries for brunch. Go wild with the decoration, and long live your appetite!

SERVES 8–10

Equipment: electric stand mixer with a dough hook

For the dough:
60g butter, plus extra for brushing
130ml whole milk
1 egg
280g strong white flour, plus extra for rolling the dough
½ tsp flaky salt
7g instant yeast
10 cardamom pods, seeds crushed to a powder, or ½ tsp ground cardamom
50g golden caster sugar

For the filling:
55g soft butter
65g light brown sugar
Zest of 1 lemon
300g fresh blueberries
2 tbsp cornflour
300g marzipan

To decorate:
3 tbsp flaked almonds
2 tbsp pearl sugar
Icing sugar, for dusting
Edible glitter
Freeze-dried raspberries

1 First, make the dough. Put the butter and milk in a small saucepan and bring to the boil to melt the butter, then remove from the heat and leave to cool to room temperature (this is important – if it is too hot it will kill the yeast). Once cool, beat in the egg.

2 Put the flour in the bowl of an electric stand mixer fitted with a dough hook, if you have one, or a large bowl if kneading by hand. Put the salt on one side of the bowl and the yeast on the other. Add the cardamom and sugar, then pour in the milk mixture. Bring everything together with your hands or the dough hook, then knead for 5–10 minutes, until you have a soft but not sticky dough (add a little more flour if it's very sticky). Cover the bowl with a tea towel and set aside to rise until doubled in size – 1–2 hours.

3 Line a large baking tray with baking parchment or a non-stick liner.

4 Tip the risen dough out onto a floured work surface and roll it to a rectangle around 40 x 30cm (16 x 12in). The long edge should be facing you.

5 Mix the butter, sugar and lemon zest for the filling together, then spread evenly over the dough using a spatula – leave a 1cm (½in) border at all edges.

continued overleaf

6 Toss the blueberries with the cornflour – this will prevent the fruit from leaking too much juice during baking – then scatter them evenly over the dough. Roll the marzipan out as thinly as possible – it is best to do this between two sheets of floured baking parchment, to avoid it sticking – to a rectangle almost the same size as the dough rectangle. Drape it over the blueberries.

7 Starting from the long edge facing you, roll the dough up as tightly as possible to form a log, tucking in the left and right ends as you roll. Transfer to the lined baking tray.

8 Using a sharp knife, cut the dough log in half horizontally, leaving it attached at just one end – so it looks like a duck's open beak. Now, take the ends of each length of dough and twist them around each other to form a braid. Form this braid into a circle (or 'crown'), pushing its ends gently together to seal. Leave in a warm place to rise for an hour.

9 Preheat the oven to 190°C fan/210°C/400°F/gas 6. Brush the dough with a little melted butter and scatter with the flaked almonds and pearl sugar. Bake for 40 minutes. Check it after 30 – if it is starting to brown too much, cover loosely with foil for the final 10 minutes.

10 Remove from the oven and leave to cool completely before dusting with icing sugar and edible glitter, and decorating with freeze-dried raspberries or decorations of your choice.

Castles crumble

This is a golden age in a dish, and it absolutely won't let you down. Sweet apricots melt under a cardamom-scented crumble topping enriched with marzipan. You can substitute peaches or plums for the apricots, and rose water or vanilla for the orange blossom water. For the full castles crumbling effect, make a half batch of the Sandcastles he destroys alfajores (page 160) and lay the unbaked cookies on top of the crumble for the final 15 minutes of baking. You'll have to crumble those castles with your spoon to get to the good stuff underneath! Build bridges rather than burning them by sharing this with your loved ones.

SERVES 4–6

Equipment: 20 x 30cm (8 x 12in) baking dish
♥ VG: use a plant-based butter alternative

1kg ripe apricots
2 tbsp runny honey
1 tbsp orange blossom water (optional)
Zest of 1 lemon and 2 tbsp juice
50g light brown sugar
½ tsp ground cardamom, or 4 whole cardamom pods, bruised
1 heaped tbsp cornflour
150g plain flour
100g cold butter, cut into cubes
40g jumbo oats
90g marzipan, cut into 5mm (¼in) cubes
90g demerara sugar
½ tsp ground cinnamon
½ tsp ground ginger
¼ tsp freshly grated nutmeg
50g chopped pistachio nuts
2 tbsp cold water or milk
Vanilla ice cream or custard, to serve

1. Preheat the oven to 170°C fan/190°C/375°F/gas 5.
2. Cut the apricots into halves, or quarters if they are very large, and remove the stones. Place the fruit in the baking dish. Add the honey, orange blossom water (if using), lemon zest and juice, light brown sugar, cardamom and cornflour. Mix well.
3. Put the flour and butter in a medium bowl. Rub the butter into the flour with your fingers until the mixture resembles breadcrumbs. Stir in the oats, marzipan, demerara sugar, cinnamon, ginger, nutmeg and pistachios and mix well. Add the cold water or milk and mix gently so the mixture turns 'pebbly'.
4. Tip the crumble over the apricots in the baking dish and spread it out to cover the fruit.
5. Bake for 45 minutes. Leave to cool for 10 minutes before serving with vanilla ice cream or custard.

RED

It's the season of autumn colours so bright, just before they lose it all. Of maple lattes clutched tightly in chilled hands, perhaps on Wednesdays in cafes. Getting lost upstate and singing in the car on a dead-end street. Red scarves and plaid shirts backdropped by the first falling snowflakes. Dwindling summer, but also new beginnings. It's trouble, treachery and being 22, burning red with passion and glowing with starlight.

There's a lot going on at the moment, so use this time to bake and break bread, to eat breakfast at midnight, and to dance around the kitchen in the light of the refrigerator as you go back for just one more piece of cake. Bring fall inside with maple and cranberries, and pay homage to holy ground with caffeinated cupcakes that'll help you take off faster than a green light. Fly to places you've never been with shamelessly decadent cake truffles that you know are absolutely no trouble at all.

Baking may be a ruthless game, but these recipes will help you to play it good and right.

KNE
WERE
TROUBLE

I KNEW YOU WERE TRUFFLES

No apologies, and no shame on you now – you don't need to explain how you've ended up with leftover cake. Just melt some chocolate, whip up a batch of cream cheese frosting and make these delightfully RED truffles (you may want to wear gloves to avoid your hands becoming stained). They're an easy way to avoid waste, and also make a beautiful contribution to a dinner party – no one will think you're trouble when you walk in carrying these. Get creative with the sprinkles – a variety of different toppings looks particularly striking. Keep them chilled (on the cold hard ground of your refrigerator) until nearly ready to eat.

MAKES AROUND 25

Equipment: cocktail stick

200g cream cheese frosting (use the recipe from page 140 Maroon velvet cake)
500g crumbled leftover cake
1 tsp red food colouring
255g dark chocolate, melted and still warm

To decorate (use some or all of the below):
Freeze-dried raspberry and/or strawberry pieces
Edible rose petals
Pink and/or red sprinkles
White chocolate stars or hearts

1 Put the cream cheese frosting, crumbled cake and food colouring in a large bowl and mix together with your hands until you have a homogenous mixture. Roll into 25 balls, each around the size of an unshelled walnut. Place the cake balls on a baking tray lined with baking parchment and chill for 30 minutes.

2 At the end of the chilling time, melt the chocolate in a heatproof bowl set over a pan of simmering water (don't let the water touch the bottom of the bowl).

3 After 30 minutes, use a cocktail stick to spear each ball and dip it into the melted chocolate to completely coat. Return the chocolate-coated balls to the baking tray and repeat until all are dipped.

4 While the chocolate is still wet, decorate the truffles as you like by sprinkling them with your chosen toppings. Return the tray to the fridge and chill and set for 30 minutes before eating.

BREAKFAST AT MIDNIGHT FLAPJACKS

It feels like the time to go out and dance as if you're 22. If you need to refuel with breakfast at midnight, pack one of these in with your dancing shoes. These British-style flapjacks are essentially granola bars, but without the pretensions of being healthy. It wouldn't be breakfast – or British – without a cup of tea, so they are also infused with the bold citrus flavours of Earl Grey. They're guaranteed to perk you up and swap your sleep for dreaming.

MAKES 16 SQUARES

Equipment: 20cm (8in) square cake tin; food processor
★ GF: use gluten-free oats
♥ VG: use a plant-based butter alternative

140g butter, plus extra for greasing the tin
130g brown sugar
2 tbsp maple syrup
A pinch of salt
35g raisins
35g dried cranberries
250g rolled oats
2 tbsp loose-leaf Earl Grey tea
20g desiccated coconut
1 tbsp sesame seeds
1 tbsp linseeds

1. Preheat the oven to 160°C fan/180°C/350°F/gas 4. Grease the tin and line with baking parchment.
2. Put the butter in a medium saucepan over a medium heat until melted. Add the brown sugar, maple syrup, salt, raisins and cranberries, stir together until syrupy, then remove from the heat. The fruit will plump up a little in the butter.
3. Put half the oats in a food processor with the Earl Grey tea leaves and blitz to a powder. Tip these into the saucepan with the butter, then add the remaining (whole) oats, coconut, sesame seeds and linseeds. Stir until well combined.
4. Tip the mixture into the prepared cake tin and level with a spoon. Bake for 22 minutes.
5. Remove the tin from the oven, leave for 5 minutes, then score out 16 squares with a sharp knife in the tin while still warm – this will help you cut them properly later.
6. Once fully cooled, transfer to a chopping board and slice into 16 squares.

LOVING HIM WAS BREAD

It's always a sad thing to break a heart. Bread, however, is absolutely made to be broken – and devoured. A homage to a love that was burning red, this loaf is packed with the reddest, most flavoursome ingredients out there: pomegranates, paprika, sumac, cranberries and beetroot. It's both sweet and savoury, ideal served with a bowl of warming soup or simply on its own with lashings of salted butter and perhaps a drizzle of honey. It'll be gone faster than the wind.

SERVES 6–8

Equipment: 25cm (10in) heart-shaped or circular cake tin (optional)

100ml rapeseed oil, plus extra for greasing the tin (optional)
100g rolled oats
2 tsp nigella seeds
2 tsp sweet smoked paprika
1 tsp ground sumac
210g spelt flour
210g plain flour
2 tsp baking powder
1 tsp bicarbonate of soda
½ tsp salt
350g grated raw beetroot
100g dried cranberries
2 eggs
1 tbsp pomegranate molasses
200g plain yoghurt
200g crumbled feta or goat's cheese

1. Preheat the oven to 200°C fan/220°C/425°F/gas 7. You can make this loaf freeform, in which case line a baking tray with baking parchment or a non-stick liner. Or grease the heart-shaped or circular cake tin and line with baking parchment.
2. Put the oats, nigella seeds, paprika, sumac, both flours, baking powder, bicarbonate of soda, salt, beetroot and cranberries in a large bowl and mix together.
3. In a large jug, whisk together the eggs, pomegranate molasses, oil and yoghurt. Pour this into the dry mixture, add the feta or goat's cheese, and mix well with your hands until the dough just comes together. It will be slightly sticky.
4. Tip the dough into the prepared tin and level it gently, or shape into a round (it helps to do this with wet hands) and place on the baking tray. Use a sharp knife to slash a deep cross into the dough – this helps it to bake evenly.
5. Bake for 40 minutes, until the loaf has risen and feels firm to the touch. Allow to cool for a few minutes (so that it's not burning red), before removing from the tray or the tin (if you used one) and transferring to a wire rack to cool.
6. This bread is best eaten fresh on the day it's made, but it also freezes well.

photographed overleaf

HOLY GROUNDS MAPLE LATTE CUPCAKES

Do you feel like having coffee and reminiscing? Put those holy grounds into these autumnal cupcakes and give fall cravings the green light – go. They have all the flavours of a maple latte, with warming cinnamon and sweet maple frosting, plus the comforting, slightly bitter note of espresso. If you want an extra-decadent treat, use a batch of the salted caramel buttercream for the no body no Daim cake on page 135 to top the cupcakes.

MAKES 12

Equipment: 12-hole cupcake tin, plus paper cases, an electric stand mixer or electric hand whisk, piping bag and nozzle, cocktail stick

For the cupcakes:
450g plain flour
1½ tsp baking powder
1 tsp bicarbonate of soda
255g light brown sugar
¾ tsp flaky salt
½ tsp ground cinnamon
150ml rapeseed oil
3 eggs
150ml hot, strong coffee (like espresso)
½ tsp vanilla extract

For the frosting:
110g soft butter
300g icing sugar, sifted
200g full-fat cream cheese
4 tbsp maple syrup
A pinch of salt

For the maple leaves and decoration:
120g orange fondant icing
Edible gold lustre

1. Preheat the oven to 180°C fan/200°C/400°F/gas 6. Line the cupcake tin with the paper cases.
2. Mix together the flour, baking powder, bicarbonate of soda, brown sugar, salt and cinnamon.
3. In a separate bowl or jug, whisk together the oil, eggs, coffee and vanilla.
4. Gently whisk the wet ingredients into the dry until just combined – don't overmix.
5. Divide the mixture between the cupcake cases. Bake for 20–25 minutes, until risen and golden. The tops of the cakes should spring back when lightly pressed with a finger. Transfer to a wire rack and leave to cool completely.
6. For the frosting, beat the butter and icing sugar together in a large bowl using an electric hand whisk or stand mixer, until well combined. Add the cream cheese, maple syrup and salt and whisk to mix thoroughly.
7. Transfer the frosting to a piping bag and pipe the frosting over each cooled cupcake into a swirl (or dollop it on with a spoon if you're feeling lazy).
8. For the maple leaves, roll out the orange fondant to around 5mm (¼in) thick. Use a cocktail stick to draw twelve maple leaves (look up a photo to help you!), then carefully cut them out using a sharp, pointed knife. Gently press a leaf into each mound of frosting on each cake. Dust with edible gold lustre to finish.

PECANS INTO PLACE

There you'll be again, in the middle of the night, dancing around the kitchen in the refrigerator light – so that you can keep coming back for more of this refrigerator cake! Everything falls together like pieces into place, in the time it'll take you to listen to 'All Too Well (10 Minute Version)' – simply melt, stir and set. It's a great one to make with children. I've added maple syrup and pecans for the perfect autumnal vibe; cosy up on those plaid shirt days with a piece of this and a spiced latte for a moment you'll remember all too well – in a good way.

MAKES 16 SQUARES

Equipment: 20cm (8in) square cake tin

★ GF: use gluten-free biscuits or cake offcuts

110g butter, plus extra for greasing
150g milk chocolate
150g dark chocolate
100g maple syrup
½ tsp flaky salt
70g dried cranberries
100g chopped pecan nuts
80g chopped dried apricots or dates
250g digestive biscuits, roughly broken up, or 250g roughly crumbled leftover cake

1 Grease the tin and line with baking parchment.

2 Put the butter, both chocolates, maple syrup and salt in a large heatproof bowl set over a pan of simmering water (don't let the water touch the bottom of the bowl). Stir regularly to melt the chocolate and butter. Once everything has melted smoothly, turn off the heat.

3 Add the rest of the ingredients (reserving 20g of the chopped pecans) to the melted mixture, mix well, then tip into the prepared tin. Scatter over the remaining chopped pecans.

4 Place in the fridge for at least 6 hours, then slice into squares to serve.

1989

This era will show you incredible things. Bold colours and even bolder drama. Flavours that jump off the plate right into your pretty face. It's all been waiting for you, a new soundtrack for dancing around your kitchen.

Have all the dates you want with a whirlwind of sugar and spice, and make it worth it for once. Get kissed by cherry lips cupcakes, drunk on gin drizzle cake or caged in caramel. Stay up with coffee at midnight and cool off with a burnt toast sundae, or experience a chocolate cake so good it's almost torture, beyond your wildest dreams. It's magic and it's madness. It's a rose garden without any thorns, just a blossoming love affair that glows in the dark. There's a blank space in your baking repertoire waiting for these recipes, and they'll never go out of style. Take a right turn and fall down a rabbit hole into a wonderland of flavours so inviting, you won't want to shake them off.

Just make sure there's someone to help you get things finally clean at the end.

COFFEE AT MIDNIGHT CAKE – WILDEST CREAMS – BURNT TOAST SUNDAE
FOXES IN BOXES COOKIES – MAGIC, MADNESS, HEAVEN, GIN
CHERRY LIPS CUPCAKES – BOYS ONLY WANT LOVE IF IT'S SACHERTORTURE
(MILK)SHAKE IT OFF PANNA COTTA

COFFEE AT MIDNIGHT CAKE

Want to stay awake to find out whether you are in love? Try this cake, which combines a healthy dose of coffee with sweet, succulent dates – a literal coffee date in cake form! It's moist, gently spiced and deliciously toffee-scented – an ideal energy boost for a late night. The sticky glaze on top makes it similar to a classic British sticky toffee pudding. Time will feel like it's moving too fast, and before you know it, every slice will be gone.

SERVES 8

Equipment: 20cm (8in) springform round cake tin, an electric stand mixer or electric hand whisk

For the cake:
150g pitted dates
240ml hot, strong coffee (like espresso)
110g soft butter, plus extra for greasing the tin
Zest of 1 orange
100g golden caster sugar
1 egg
235g plain flour
2 tsp baking powder
1 tsp ground cinnamon
½ tsp ground ginger
¼ tsp freshly grated nutmeg

For the glaze and decoration:
50g butter
50g light brown sugar
50g dark brown sugar
2 tbsp strong coffee
14 pecan nuts
Edible silver lustre

1 Set aside twelve of the dates. Roughly chop the others and put in a bowl with the hot coffee. Leave for 20 minutes.

2 Preheat the oven to 180°C fan/200°C/400°F/gas 6. Grease the cake tin and line with baking parchment.

3 Meanwhile, put the butter, orange zest and golden caster sugar in a large bowl, or the bowl of an electric stand mixer, and cream together using the mixer or an electric hand whisk for 3–5 minutes, until light and fluffy. Add the egg and beat to incorporate, then add the date and coffee mixture and mix well. Add the flour, baking powder, cinnamon, ginger and nutmeg, then mix gently to a smooth batter.

4 Pour the batter into the prepared tin. Arrange the whole dates round the edge at even intervals, like the twelve numbers on a clock.

5 Bake for 35 minutes, until risen and the centre of the cake springs back when pressed lightly with a finger. Set aside to cool while you make the glaze.

6 Put the butter, both sugars and the coffee in a saucepan and bring to the boil, stirring to melt the butter. Simmer for 2–3 minutes, until thick and syrupy. Set aside for 2–3 minutes to thicken slightly, then pour over the cake.

7 Arrange the pecan nuts around the cake, putting one on top of each date. Finally, arrange a short line of the remaining pecans from the middle of the cake upwards, like the '12' hand on a clock. Once the glaze has set, spray or paint the pecan nuts with edible silver lustre.

WILDEST CREAMS

Say you'll remember this delicious set custard. It's a dream come true, infused with rooibos tea from South Africa, where the 'Wildest Dreams' video was filmed. This lends it an unusual, slightly honeyed note (Earl Grey and jasmine tea leaves work well too). You'll be burning it down when you caramelise the sugary topping to get a delicious crunchy crust that yields gently to your spoon. It won't last forever – nothing does – but the few moments you spend savouring this will be pretty good now. It's a great make-ahead dessert – all you need to do at the last minute is caramelise the top.

MAKES 4

Equipment: 4 ramekins (around 10cm/4in in diameter and at least 3cm/1¼in high); a cook's blowtorch (optional, but useful); food thermometer (optional, but useful)
★ GF

240ml whole milk
240ml double cream
4 rooibos tea bags
4 egg yolks
65g caster sugar
½ tsp flaky salt
2 tsp icing sugar

1. Put the milk and cream into a large saucepan and bring to the boil. Add the tea bags and remove from the heat. Set aside for 20–30 minutes to infuse.
2. Meanwhile, whisk the egg yolks, sugar and salt together in a large bowl until thickened and slightly paler in colour – about 3–5 minutes.
3. Remove the teabags from the milk and cream. Pour a third of the milk and cream into the egg yolk mixture, whisking as you go. Then pour the rest in, whisk well, and tip the lot back into the saucepan.
4. Preheat the oven to 160°C fan/180°C/350°F/gas 4.
5. Put the saucepan over a medium-low heat and whisk constantly until the mixture thickens enough to coat the back of a spoon. Don't put the heat too high or the eggs will scramble. The temperature should reach 71°C (160°F), if you have a food thermometer. Remove from the heat.
6. Line a deep oven tray with a clean tea towel and place four ramekins on the tea towel. Boil a kettle full of water.
7. Divide the custard between the ramekins. Pour the boiled water into the oven tray so that it reaches halfway up the sides of the ramekins (this helps to cook the custard evenly).
8. Bake for 25–30 minutes, until the custard is mostly set but still has a slight wobble (it will set more as it cools). Remove from the oven, leave to cool for 15 minutes, then place in the fridge for at least 3 hours.
9. Once chilled, dust the icing sugar over the top of each ramekin and either use a cook's blowtorch or place the ramekins under a hot grill for 2–3 minutes to caramelise it. Serve immediately.

BURNT TOAST SUNDAE

Relive lazy Sunday mornings by falling in love with this cosy confection, full of the flavours of breakfast in bed. Brown bread ice cream is one of those peculiarly British things that sounds odd but tastes great, particularly if you make it using a good loaf, dense with whole grains and seeds. It requires advance planning but is very easy (and not actually burnt – just pleasantly caramelised). You don't need an ice cream maker, though the result will be smoother if you do use one. Layer the ice cream up with fresh raspberries and raspberry coulis for toast-and-jam in a glass. It's delicious – you can hear it in the silence that will follow.

SERVES 4

Equipment: ice cream maker (optional, but useful)

♥ VG: use plant-based butter and double cream alternatives

For the brown bread ice cream (makes just over ½ litre):
55g butter
100g dark brown sugar
1 tsp ground cinnamon
¼ tsp ground nutmeg
80g brown breadcrumbs (from a dense, multigrain loaf is best)
500ml double cream
80g golden caster sugar
½ tsp flaky salt
1 tsp vanilla extract

For the sundae:
200g fresh raspberries
8 tbsp shop-bought raspberry coulis

1. Melt the butter in a medium saucepan and add the dark brown sugar, spices and breadcrumbs. Cook over a medium heat, stirring, for 3–5 minutes, until the crumbs are buttery and fragrant. Turn off the heat and leave to cool completely.
2. Whip the double cream with the caster sugar, salt and vanilla until just holding its shape. Stir through the buttery, spiced breadcrumbs.
3. Churn in an ice cream machine, if you have one, or place in a container in the freezer and whisk every hour for 4 hours to break up any ice crystals. Chill in the freezer for at least 6 hours before serving.
4. To serve, layer scoops of the ice cream in four sundae glasses with the fresh raspberries and raspberry coulis.

FOXES IN BOXES COOKIES

You'd better hide these cookies in places they won't be found, because they're so cute that everyone will want to hunt them down and put them in boxes. I use an embossed cookie cutter from Birkmann, but if you can't find the exact same one, simply decorate the foxes according to the pattern of your own cutter. To really give the 'I Know Places' vibe, put some of your foxes in cages made of caramel – they take some practice to make (you'll be chasing your tail for a bit), but they are easier than you might think and really give a wow factor.

MAKES AROUND 18, DEPENDING ON THE SIZE OF YOUR CUTTER

Equipment: electric stand mixer or electric hand whisk, fox-shaped cookie cutter

For the cookies:
190g soft butter
125g golden caster sugar
2 eggs, beaten
Zest of 1 orange
312g plain flour, plus extra for rolling the dough
1 tsp baking powder
½ tsp flaky salt

To decorate:
225g orange fondant icing
Edible glue (or 2 tbsp apricot jam, warmed in a pan with a splash of water until syrupy)
3–4 tbsp sprinkles (for the tails)
Black liquid icing pen

For the caramel cages (makes 8–12):
200g sugar

1 Cream the butter and sugar together in an electric stand mixer or using an electric hand whisk for 5 minutes, until light and fluffy. Beat in the eggs, a little at a time. Add the orange zest, flour, baking powder and salt, and beat gently until the mixture just comes together. Shape into a rough ball, wrap in baking parchment and chill in the fridge for 1 hour.

2 Preheat the oven to 170°C fan/190°C/375°F/gas 5. Line two baking trays with baking parchment or a non-stick liner.

3 On a floured work surface, roll out the dough to around 5mm (¼in) thick. Use your cookie cutter to cut out fox shapes, then place them on the prepared baking trays with at least 5cm (2in) of space between them. Re-roll any offcuts and cut out more cookies until all the dough is used up.

4 Bake for 10–13 minutes, until light golden brown. Leave to cool completely on a wire rack.

5 To decorate, roll out your orange fondant to a thickness of around 3mm (⅛in), then use the same fox cookie cutter to cut out shapes to top the cookies. Brush the cookies with the edible glue or jam and stick a fox-shaped piece of fondant on top of each cookie.

6 Use more edible glue or jam to stick on the sprinkles, then draw on the details using a black icing pen.

continued overleaf

7 For the caramel cages, put the sugar in a medium saucepan over a high heat. The sugar will begin to melt at the edges, so swirl the pan to help it melt evenly, but do not stir. Once all the sugar has melted and started to turn golden, lower the heat to medium and cook for another 30 seconds or so, until you have a deep golden caramel. Watch it like a hawk (or a fox) – it can burn in seconds – and swirl occasionally if it looks like it is catching. Immediately turn off the heat.

8 Wait about a minute for the caramel in the pan to cool slightly, then drizzle a little of it over the back of a ladle with a wooden spoon to create a cage pattern (this takes some practice!). Now wait for 30–60 seconds for the caramel to be cool enough to touch but not harden completely – be careful not to burn yourself. Gently peel the caramel cage off the ladle – it should be pliable enough – and immediately shape it back into a dome with your hands, then set aside to cool and harden. Repeat with the remaining caramel – if it hardens too much in the pan, gently heat to bring it back to a more liquid stage.

9 Serve the cookies on a large plate with a few caramel cages placed over some of the foxes. Find a place where you won't be found to enjoy them!

MAGIC, MADNESS, HEAVEN, GIN

Oh my god, look at that cake – does it look like your next mistake? No, because it's wonderfully easy, and baking it is a game that you'll definitely want to play. This is based on a classic British lemon drizzle cake, but (My Version) bursts with the fresh flavours of a gin and tonic. An incredible thing, I'm sure you'll agree. It's enough to make even the baddest guys good for a weekend. Feel free to leave out the gin if baking for children or non-drinkers – or replace it with your favourite non-alcoholic spirit.

MAKES 1 LARGE LOAF CAKE OR 2 SMALLER ONES

Equipment: 900g (2lb) loaf tin or two 450g (1lb) loaf tins, an electric stand mixer or electric hand whisk, cocktail stick

225g golden caster sugar
Zest of 2 limes, juice of 1
220g soft butter, plus extra for greasing the tin(s)
4 eggs, beaten
225g self-raising flour
A pinch of salt
80g caster sugar
2 tbsp gin (optional)

1. Preheat the oven to 160°C fan/180°C/350°F/gas 4. Grease your loaf tin(s) and line with baking parchment.
2. Put the golden caster sugar and lime zest in a large bowl and rub together with your fingers to release the fragrant oils. Add the butter and, using an electric hand whisk, cream together for 3–5 minutes, until light and fluffy. You can also do this in a stand mixer. Gradually add the eggs, a little at a time, beating after each addition. Add the flour and salt and mix gently to form a smooth batter.
3. Pour the batter into the prepared tin(s) and bake for 50–60 minutes if making one large loaf, or 35–40 minutes if making two smaller loaves, until golden brown and the top of the cake springs back when gently pressed with a finger.
4. Remove the cake(s) from the oven. Using a cocktail stick, prick holes all over the cake(s). In a small bowl, whisk together the lime juice, caster sugar and gin (if using). Spoon this mixture all over the surface of the cake(s) so that it drizzles into the holes. Leave to cool completely before eating.

CHERRY LIPS CUPCAKES

You can show your guests incredible things with these cupcakes. They're irresistibly pink and packed with cherry flavour – a perfect storm of delicious ingredients coming together, with no screaming and crying whatsoever (unless you get drunk on jealousy over who gets to eat the last one). You can buy morello cherry purée in sachets for making cocktails, or you could swap this for cherry jam or raspberry coulis if you can't find it. Serve on a platter under crystal skies and I guarantee that, pretty soon, there will be just a blank space left.

MAKES 12

Equipment: electric stand mixer or electric hand whisk, lips-shaped cookie cutter, 12-hole cupcake tin and paper cases, a piping bag (optional, but useful)

For the cakes:
185g soft butter
225g golden caster sugar
3 eggs, beaten
225g plain yoghurt
½ tsp pink food colouring
240g plain flour
½ tsp baking powder
½ tsp salt
1½ tsp vanilla extract
225g fresh cherries, halved and pitted, or fresh raspberries
½ tbsp cornflour

For the frosting and decoration:
170g soft butter
320g icing sugar
8 tbsp morello cherry purée, or 4 tbsp cherry jam
120g pink fondant icing
12 cocktail cherries in syrup, or fresh cherries with stalks on, if in season
3 tbsp each freeze-dried raspberry pieces and white chocolate stars, for sprinkling

1. Line your cupcake tin with paper cases. Preheat the oven to 180°C fan/200°C/400°F/gas 6.
2. Using a stand mixer or electric hand whisk, cream the butter and sugar together for 3–5 minutes, until very light and fluffy. Add the eggs, a little at a time, beating between each addition, until fully incorporated. Add the yoghurt and food colouring and mix well. Fold in the flour, baking powder, salt and vanilla until you have a smooth mixture – don't overmix.
3. Toss the cherries (or raspberries) with the cornflour in a small bowl – this will prevent them sinking to the bottom of the cakes during baking. Fold the fruit through the cake mixture, then divide the mix between the paper cases.
4. Bake for 20–22 minutes, until the cakes are golden and the tops spring back when lightly pressed in the centre with a finger. Remove to a wire rack and leave to cool completely before decorating.
5. For the frosting, beat together the butter and icing sugar with an electric mixer or hand whisk until thick and fluffy. Add the cherry purée or jam and whisk again briefly to incorporate. Transfer the frosting to a piping bag and pipe it onto the centre of each cupcake (or use a spoon).
6. Roll out the pink fondant to around 5mm (¼in) thick and cut out lip shapes. Place a pair of fondant lips onto the frosting of each cupcake. Place a cocktail cherry into the frosting next to the lips.
7. Sprinkle freeze-dried raspberries and white chocolate stars over the remaining frosting on each cake.

BOYS ONLY WANT LOVE IF IT'S SACHERTORTURE

This one's for the Vienna Swifties, who sadly never got to have their Eras Tour moment in 2024. I was one of them, and I coped by drowning my sorrows in the very best cake Vienna has to offer: the classic Sachertorte. This decadent combination of dark chocolate sponge, apricot jam and chocolate ganache is deservedly world-famous. This is (My Version), which adds a little more texture in the form of juicy dried apricots in the filling.

SERVES 10–12

Equipment: 25cm (10in) heart-shaped cake tin, an electric stand mixer or electric hand whisk

For the cake:
180g butter, plus extra for greasing
200g dark chocolate
7 eggs, separated
180g caster sugar
A pinch of salt
50g light brown sugar
175g plain flour
30g ground almonds

For the filling:
225g apricot jam
80g dried apricots, finely chopped
2 tbsp apricot brandy or liqueur, orange juice or water

For the glaze and decoration:
200g dark chocolate
70g butter
75ml double cream
200g fresh raspberries

1 Preheat the oven to 170°C fan/190°C/375°F/gas 5. Grease the base and sides of your cake tin and line with baking parchment.

2 Melt the chocolate in a heatproof bowl set over a pan of simmering water (don't let the water touch the bottom of the bowl). Once melted, set aside to cool slightly.

3 Using a stand mixer or electric hand whisk, whip the egg whites to stiff peaks, then gradually add the caster sugar and salt, whisking until you have a firm meringue.

4 In another bowl, using a stand mixer or electric hand whisk, whisk together the butter and light brown sugar until pale and fluffy. Whisk in the egg yolks, one at a time, then stir in the melted chocolate, flour and ground almonds until combined.

5 Using a large metal spoon, take a quarter of the meringue mixture and fold it, using a circular motion, into the chocolate mixture to loosen it. Once it is incorporated, fold in the rest of the meringue mixture, being careful not to knock out the air.

6 Tip the mixture into the prepared cake tin and bake for around 40 minutes, until risen and the cake springs back when gently pressed on top with a finger. Set aside to cool completely.

continued overleaf

7 Place the apricot jam, dried apricots and brandy or alternative in a medium saucepan and bring gently to the boil, stirring. Lower the heat and simmer for 5 minutes, until slightly thickened and syrupy. Set aside.

8 Once the cake is completely cool, use a serrated knife to slice it in half horizontally. Spread most of the apricot mixture over the cut side of the bottom half – make sure all the pieces of dried apricot are on the cake, but leave about 2 tablespoons of the syrup behind in the pan. Sandwich the other cake half on top of the apricot jam, then brush the cake all over with the remaining syrup from the pan.

9 For the glaze, melt the dark chocolate and butter in a heatproof bowl set over a pan of simmering water (don't let the water touch the bottom of the bowl). Once melted, remove from the heat and whisk in the cream to make a loose chocolate ganache. Spread this all over the cake using a palette knife. Place raspberries all around the edge of the cake. Leave to set for an hour before serving.

(MILK)SHAKE IT OFF PANNA COTTA

This panna cotta can't stop, won't stop moving to its own sick beat. You can shake it off for as long as you like before digging in – though you probably won't want to wait long. Inspired by the flavours of a strawberry milkshake, it's paired with a fresh and fruity strawberry compote that marries beautifully with the delicate vanilla cream. If you've never tried black pepper with strawberries before, prepare to love the way its gentle heat brings out the best of the berries' sweetness. You can also try pink peppercorns, if you can find them, which give a delightful sherbetty tingle and are beautiful to behold.

SERVES 4

Equipment: 4 dariole moulds or ramekins

★ GF

For the panna cotta:
300ml double cream
160ml whole milk
50g caster sugar
1 vanilla pod, split down the centre
Neutral-tasting oil such as vegetable or groundnut, for greasing
3 gelatine sheets (around 5g)

For the compote:
240g fresh strawberries, hulled and quartered
½ tsp vanilla extract
A good grind of black pepper or 1 tsp pink peppercorns, lightly crushed

1 Put the cream, milk, sugar and vanilla pod in a medium saucepan and bring to just below the boil. Turn off the heat, cover with a lid and leave to infuse for 1 hour.

2 Strain the mixture through a fine sieve into a jug, pressing the vanilla pod into the sieve with the back of a spoon to extract all the flavour. (You can rinse and dry the pod, then place it in a jar of sugar to scent it – waste not want not!) Return the mixture to the pan.

3 Very lightly grease 4 dariole moulds or ramekins with the oil.

4 Fill a small jug with cold water. Place the gelatine sheets in the water for 2–3 minutes to soften, then gently squeeze the water out of them with your hands. Put them into the pan with the milk and cream mixture, then heat gently, stirring with a wooden spoon, until the gelatine has dissolved.

5 Divide the mixture between the four moulds or ramekins, then place in the fridge for at least a couple of hours, until set but still with a slight wobble.

6 While the panna cotta sets, make the compote. Simply stir together all the ingredients in a bowl then set aside for the flavours to infuse. The strawberries will become delightfully juicy.

7 When ready to serve, briefly dip the underside of each mould or ramekin into a bowl of hot water (around 20–30 seconds – you don't want to melt the panna cotta!) to loosen the mixture slightly, then place an upside-down plate on top and flip over. The panna cotta should slide out. Spoon the strawberry compote over the top of each panna cotta, then serve immediately.

Reputation

There will be no explanation, there will be just sweet creation.

If baking is your end game, these recipes are your A-team. They are sweet and savoury, and will fly you all around the world, drawing on influences from China to Morocco – unlike a getaway car, they'll take you pretty far. Donut blame me if you keep slithering back for more snake cake, or use the money in your bag to buy more butter for a caramel shortbread that's the one you've been waiting for. Feel like you're riding a jet stream as you create an effortless autumnal appetiser that'll keep you warm without the need to build a fire or burn your bridges. For a succulent snack you won't regret, and will want to make over and over, try your hand at a batch of fluffy pandan-scented sweet buns. Or make a mess – but a mess that you certainly won't have a bad feeling about.

Call it whatever you want – but I reckon you'll be calling it delicious.

Snake cake

Don't wait until international snake day to enjoy this beauty – it's a delightful treat all year round. It's based on the Moroccan pastry m'hencha, which is made of warqa dough (similar to filo pastry), filled with sweetened ground almonds and drenched in a fragrant syrup – a little like baklava. In a nod to another well-known story about a woman and a snake, I've used apple in the filling here. Rolling up the pastry is a little delicate, but it's quite forgiving. Don't worry too much about any gaps or breakages – the end effect will still be sssssspectacular.

SERVES 8–10

Equipment: 20cm (8in) round cake tin without a removable base

For the pastry:
110g melted butter, plus extra for greasing and brushing
8 sheets filo pastry

For the filling:
120g dried apple rings
50g pitted dates or sultanas
1 tsp ground cinnamon
Zest of 1 lemon
150g ground almonds
A pinch of salt
2 egg yolks

For the syrup:
85g honey
65g caster sugar
60ml water
1 tsp rose water

To decorate:
15g pink fondant icing (for the tongue)
2 edible googly eyes
Coloured icing pens

1 Put all the filling ingredients, except the egg yolks, in a food processor and blitz until everything is chopped very finely. Add the egg yolks and pulse until the mixture clumps together. Divide into four equal portions and set aside.

2 Grease the cake tin with a little of the melted butter. Preheat the oven to 180°C fan/200°C/400°F/gas 6.

3 Keep the filo pastry sheets covered with a damp tea towel while you work, so that they don't dry out. Take one sheet and lay it, short side facing you, on a work surface. Brush it liberally with melted butter. Take another sheet and lay it on top, then brush that with butter too.

4 Take one of the portions of filling and use your hands to shape it into a sausage 2.5cm (1in) wide. Lay it along the bottom of the filo sheet facing you, almost to the edges.

5 Start to roll the filo up over the sausage filling, tucking in the ends of the pastry as you go. Roll it tightly but allow the filo to bunch and scrunch a little, to prevent it cracking later on. Once you have a rolled sausage of filo, coil it tightly on itself into a spiral shape and place it in the centre of the greased cake tin. Brush liberally with melted butter.

continued overleaf

6 Repeat this step three more times with the remaining sheets of filo and filling. Each time you complete a sausage, spiral it tightly in the tin, starting from the end of the previous coil, so that you're making a spiral that gets larger each time. Brush each part with melted butter. You should end up with a spiral that fits neatly into the cake tin. Brush with more melted butter, then bake for 30–40 minutes, until golden all over.

7 Put the honey, caster sugar and water into a small saucepan and bring to the boil, stirring to melt the honey. Simmer for 5 minutes, until thickened slightly. Remove from the heat and add the rose water. (You can make the syrup in advance, but you will need to reheat it before use as it needs to be hot when poured over the cake.)

8 Once the cake has baked, immediately pour the warm syrup over the top and allow it to soak in. Leave to cool completely.

9 Once cool, shape the snake's tongue out of pink fondant and attach it to the end of the spiral. Place the two googly eyes near the tongue to form a face. Now decorate the cake however you wish, with coloured icing pens – I drew zig-zag lines in red and green.

Donut blame me

Donut freak out: these donuts are baked rather than fried. It means they're slightly healthier, so you can justify coming back for another! Golden with luxurious daisy-yellow saffron and decorated with edible wafer daisies and (fondant) poison ivy leaves, they're almost intoxicatingly good. I shape these with a circular cookie cutter and bake them freeform, but you could use a specialist donut mould for perfect uniform shapes.

MAKES 13

Equipment: an electric stand mixer or electric hand whisk, circular cookie cutter, around 6.5cm (2½in) in diameter, shot glass or small round cutter, ivy leaf cutter (optional)

For the donuts:
320ml whole milk
90g butter
A generous pinch of saffron strands
2 eggs
200g golden caster sugar
700g plain flour, plus extra for rolling and shaping the dough
1 tsp flaky salt
7g instant yeast

For the icing:
240g icing sugar, sifted
1 tsp yellow food colouring

For the decoration:
150g green fondant icing
12 edible wafer daisies

1. Place the milk and half the butter in a small saucepan and bring to the boil. Once boiling, add the saffron and remove from the heat. Set aside to cool to room temperature (this is important, as otherwise you'll kill the yeast). Once cool, whisk in the eggs.
2. Put the sugar and flour in a large mixing bowl or the bowl of a stand mixer fitted with a dough hook. Put the salt and yeast on different sides of the bowl. Add the milk mixture, then bring together into a soft dough using your hands or the mixer. Knead for 5–10 minutes, until soft and silky but not sticky – add a little extra flour if it sticks too much. Cover the bowl with a tea towel and set aside until the dough has doubled in size – around 1–2 hours.
3. Line two baking trays with baking parchment or non-stick liners.
4. Once the dough has risen, tip it onto a lightly floured work surface and roll it out to a thickness of around 2.5cm (1in).
5. Using the circular cutter, cut out 13 circles of dough. Place them gently on the prepared baking trays, at least 7.5cm (3in) apart. Use an upturned shot glass or similar to cut smaller circles out of the centre of the dough circles. (You can form all the tiny circles of dough into one more big circle, then cut one final hole out of it – discard this final 'hole', or bake it and eat it as a cook's perk!)

continued overleaf

6 Preheat the oven to 190°C fan/210°C/400°F/gas 6. Leave the donuts to rise for another 30–45 minutes – they will puff up slightly. Melt the remaining butter in a small saucepan and set aside.

7 Bake for 8–10 minutes, until the donuts are golden brown. Remove from the oven and immediately brush each donut with the melted butter. Leave to cool completely on a wire rack before decorating.

8 For the icing, mix together the icing sugar in a large bowl with the food colouring and just enough water to make a stiff mixture – about 1–2 tablespoons.

9 Spoon the icing thickly over each donut and spread it all over the top with the back of a spoon.

10 Roll out the green fondant icing to 5mm (¼in) thick and cut out leaf shapes using a cutter, or freehand with a sharp knife (you can use a photo of poison ivy as a guide). Decorate each donut with leaves and an edible wafer daisy.

Call it what you wontons

Do you recall late November? It's time for Thanksgiving, and nearly Christmas, and these sweet-savoury wonton-shaped pastries are a perfect appetiser for autumnal dinner gatherings. They can be adapted to suit your taste and the contents of your fridge – use jam if you want something sweet, or a more savoury chutney for a tangier, saltier kick. Call them, and make them, what you want! My favourite filling is fig chutney, but these also work very well with cranberry sauce or British mincemeat.

MAKES 12

♥ VG: use plant-based cheese and butter alternatives

340g full-fat cream cheese or soft goat's cheese
1 tbsp cornflour
2 tsp chopped thyme leaves
80g roughly chopped pecan nuts
A pinch of salt
9 sheets filo pastry
85g melted butter
8 tbsp cranberry sauce, jam or chutney
Honey or maple syrup, to drizzle (optional)

1. Whisk together the cheese, cornflour, thyme, pecans and salt. Set aside.
2. Preheat the oven to 190°C fan/210°C/400°F/gas 6.
3. Take one sheet of filo pastry and lay it on your worktop. Keep the other sheets covered with a damp tea towel to prevent them drying out.
4. Brush the filo sheet with melted butter, then flip it over so the buttery side is on the worktop (this keeps the filo pliable). Brush the dry side with butter. Layer another sheet over the top and brush this with butter too, then another sheet, again brushing with butter (so you have three sheets on top of each other). Cut this into four squares. Set the squares aside under the damp towel and take the remaining (dry) filo.
5. Repeat with the remaining six filo sheets, so you end up with twelve squares of filo.
6. Divide the cream cheese filling between each square, dolloping it in the middle and pressing it down gently with a spoon.
7. Spoon a tablespoon of the sauce, jam or chutney onto each dollop of cream cheese filling.
8. Gather the edges of the filo up around the filling, pinching them shut at the top and twisting very gently to seal. Brush each parcel with melted butter and lay on a greased and lined baking tray.
9. Bake for 25–30 minutes, until golden brown. Leave to cool for 5 minutes before serving, drizzled with the honey or maple syrup, if liked.

The (Emperor's) mess that you wanted

This recipe combines two of the greatest culinary messes in history. Eton Mess is a classic British dessert of strawberries, meringue and whipped cream. Kaiserschmarrn, which translates as 'Emperor's Mess', is an Austrian dish that was a favourite of the Emperor (Kaiser) Franz Joseph I. It's a fluffy pancake, studded with rum-soaked raisins, that is shredded and then caramelised in butter and sugar and served with apple or plum compote. This kaiserschmarrn is accompanied by strawberries and whipped cream, Etonian style. It's delicious for brunch or dessert – in which case you'll probably want to serve a smaller portion.

SERVES 4–6 GENEROUSLY

Equipment: electric stand mixer or electric hand whisk, a large ovenproof frying pan, around 23cm (9in) in diameter

2 tbsp rum, orange juice or water
2 tbsp raisins or sultanas
4 eggs, separated
¼ tsp salt
3 tbsp caster sugar
200ml milk
145g plain flour
1 tsp vanilla extract
Zest of 1 lemon
4 tbsp butter
2 tbsp light brown sugar
400g strawberries
2 tbsp icing sugar
Whipped cream, to serve

1 Put the rum, orange juice or water in a small saucepan and bring to the boil. Add the raisins or sultanas, turn off the heat, and leave for 15 minutes, until plumped up.

2 Preheat the oven to 180°C fan/200°C/400°F/gas 6.

3 Put the egg whites in the bowl of an electric stand mixer or a large bowl. Beat using the mixer or an electric hand whisk until soft peaks form. Add the salt and caster sugar, and beat again for 30 seconds to incorporate.

4 In a separate large bowl, whisk the egg yolks and milk together, then sift in the flour. Whisk vigorously until you have a lump-free batter. Add the vanilla and lemon zest, then stir in the raisins or sultanas and any leftover liquid.

5 Using a large metal spoon, add a quarter of the egg white mixture to the milk batter. Fold it gently into the batter with a curving motion to lighten the batter. Add the remaining egg white mixture and fold until incorporated – do not overmix.

6 Heat half the butter in the frying pan over a medium-high heat. Once melted, swirl to coat the base and sides of the pan, then pour in the batter. Lower the heat to medium and cook for 3 minutes. Turn off the heat and place the pan in the oven.

7 Bake for 12–15 minutes, until the pancake is puffed up, firm and lightly golden on top. Remove from the oven.

continued overleaf

8 Use a wooden spatula to roughly break the pancake into lots of small pieces – there's no need to be precise; the more rough and uneven the pieces are, the better. Tip the pancake pieces into a large bowl.

9 Return the empty pan to the hob and add the remaining butter. Heat over a medium heat until the butter is foaming, then add the light brown sugar. Return the pancake pieces to the pan. Stir to coat them in the buttery sugar, then cook for 3–5 minutes. Stir occasionally but not too often – you want them to caramelise at the edges.

10 Remove the pan from the heat. Hull and halve the strawberries and scatter them over the pancake pieces in the pan. Dust everything with the icing sugar and serve, with whipped cream on the side.

Getaway car-amel slices

It's the best of times when you've got a piece of this in front of you. This recipe is based on a classic millionaire's shortbread, but with a twist of orange and whisky in homage to the Old Fashioned that started it all. It's got enough sugar to fuel any quick getaway, and you won't want to leave a single piece behind at the motel.

MAKES 20 SMALL PIECES

Equipment: 28 x 18cm (11 x 7in) traybake tin

For the shortbread base:
220g soft butter, plus extra for greasing the tin
100g caster sugar
280g plain flour
2 tsp baking powder

For the caramel:
180g butter
175g caster sugar
2 tbsp golden syrup
400g can condensed milk
Zest of ½ orange
¼ tsp flaky salt
1 tbsp whisky (optional)

For the chocolate topping:
300g orange-flavoured dark chocolate

1. Preheat the oven to 160°C fan/180°C/350°F/gas 4. Grease your tin and line with baking parchment.
2. Using a food processor or a wooden spoon, mix together the soft butter, caster sugar, flour and baking powder. Tip into the lined tin and press together into an even layer using the back of a spoon. Prick all over with a fork.
3. Bake for 40 minutes, until light golden brown.
4. Meanwhile, make the caramel. Put the butter, sugar, golden syrup, condensed milk, orange zest and salt into a large saucepan and bring to the boil over a medium heat, stirring to help the butter melt. Let the mixture simmer for 5–10 minutes, stirring constantly, until it becomes light brown and thickens so that it pulls away from the sides of the pan as you stir – it will reach 102°C (216°F) on a thermometer. Remove from the heat once it has reached this stage, and stir in the whisky (if using).
5. Once the shortbread base has baked, leave it to cool for around 10 minutes, then pour over the caramel mixture (you may need to warm it up if it has stiffened too much) and smooth it over the top. Leave to set for around 15 minutes.
6. Break the chocolate into even pieces and put in a heatproof bowl over a pan of simmering water (don't let the water touch the bottom of the bowl). Stir regularly until it has completely melted.
7. Pour the chocolate over the caramel layer, smoothing it with a palette knife or spatula. Leave to cool, then put in the fridge for 30 minutes or so to firm up before slicing with a hot knife into 20 pieces.

I dim sum-thing bad

Why do these feel so good? Perhaps because eating these pillowy clouds of custard-stuffed dough is some of the most fun you'll ever have. Custard buns often feature in the Cantonese tradition of dim sum (small plates) enjoyed with tea (cha). I've Rep-coded these with the green custard – the green comes from pandan, a fragrant leaf used in south-east Asian cooking, with a flavour somewhere between cooked rice, coconut and vanilla. You can find it in Asian groceries or online, but you could also swap it for vanilla and some green food colouring instead.

MAKES 6

Equipment: electric stand mixer with a dough hook, a bamboo or metal steamer

For the pandan custard:
1 egg and 1 egg yolk
30g icing sugar
100ml whole milk
30ml double cream
35g cornflour
30g butter
1 tsp pandan extract
A pinch of salt

For the dough:
140g plain flour
1 tsp instant yeast
2 tbsp caster sugar
1 tbsp rapeseed oil
A pinch of salt
90ml whole milk

1. For the custard, put everything in a small saucepan and heat gently, whisking constantly. Raise the heat to medium, then keep whisking, for 2–5 minutes, until the mixture stands in thick peaks when you remove the whisk. Decant it into a clean bowl. Set aside to cool, then place in the fridge, covered with cling film.
2. For the dough, place all the ingredients in the bowl of a stand mixer fitted with a dough hook, or a large bowl if kneading by hand. Bring everything together into a rough dough and knead for 10 minutes, until soft but not sticky. Cover the bowl with a tea towel and leave to rise until doubled in size – around 1–2 hours.
3. Once the dough has risen, divide it into six equal balls. Roll out each ball into a flat circle around 5mm (¼in) thick. Divide the custard into six balls, too, using your hands – it should be firm enough. Place a ball of custard in the centre of each dough circle, then bring the dough up around the ball and pinch together to seal it. Twist the seal and roll the dough ball gently between your hands to shape and seal it completely. Place on a baking tray lined with baking parchment or a non-stick liner. Repeat with the remaining dough and custard.
4. Leave the dough balls for 30–60 minutes, until increased in size by half.
5. Cut six small squares of baking parchment for each bun to sit on. Place each bun on a piece of paper in the rack of a bamboo or metal steamer.
6. Steam the buns over a pan of simmering water for 10 minutes. After 10 minutes, turn off the heat and leave for another 5 minutes before opening the steamer and serving.

Be ready for combat in the kitchen without any invisible smoke, and make easy prey of these recipes that you'll definitely want to save a seat for at every table. If you like shiny things, you'll love this era of soft pastels, golden daylight, dazzling hazes and blessed rains. It's time for sacred new beginnings, and what better way to worship a new love than with sweetness and sparkle?

It's your place, you make the rules, and who says you can't bake a cake like a rainbow with all of the colours? Brighten up the cruellest summer with a delicious dark berry pudding that's bluer than an icy outdoor pool, or make nice friends with friands. Swap your heartbreak prince for a Linzer torte that's red or blue, depending on how you roll the dice.

This era is a celebration of love, so bake, give, eat and let's meet in the afterglow.

ME! rainbow layer cake

I promise that you'll never find another like this cake. It's spectacularly fun (like spelling!) to bake and serve at a birthday party or gathering. You can buy specialist kits of food colouring and tins designed to make rainbow layer cakes, so look out for those to help you. If you don't have seven cake tins, or your oven isn't big enough to bake seven cakes at once, you can use two or three tins and bake the cakes in batches. Decorate with edible friendship bracelets spelling out a message of your choice – or leave undecorated and wait for the surprise when your guests cut that first slice!

SERVES 10–12

Equipment: seven 15cm (6in) round cake tins, ideally springform, an electric stand mixer or electric hand whisk

For the cakes:
360g soft butter, plus extra for greasing
360g caster sugar
1 tsp flaky salt
5 eggs, beaten
80g plain yoghurt
45ml milk
360g self-raising flour
½ tsp baking powder
½–1 tsp each of red, orange, yellow, green, blue, indigo and violet food colouring (pastes or gels are generally better than liquids)

For the buttercream:
330g soft butter
560g icing sugar, sifted
Food colouring in a colour of your choice

For the friendship bracelet decoration (optional):
Edible beads in colours of your choice (buy these online or make them out of coloured fondant icing)
100g readymade white fondant icing
Black edible ink pen

1 Preheat the oven to 170°C fan/190°C/375°F/gas 5. Grease your cake tins and line with baking parchment.

2 Beat the butter, sugar and salt using an electric hand whisk or stand mixer until light and fluffy – about 3–5 minutes. Gradually add the eggs, whisking well between each addition. Once the eggs are all whisked in, add the yoghurt and milk and mix again briefly. Finally, add the flour and baking powder and mix just enough to combine.

3 Weigh the mixture, then divide by seven – place each portion of the mixture in an individual bowl. Add a different colour of food colouring to each bowl – add each colour gradually, drop by drop or bit by bit, whisking it in gently until you get a bright, bold colour. You should now have seven bowls of mixture in all the colours of the rainbow.

4 Spoon the mixtures into the prepared tins, with one colour in each. (If baking the cakes in batches, do 2 or 3 colours at a time, leaving the remaining mixtures to one side while the other cakes bake.)

5 Bake for 20–25 minutes, until the cakes are risen and golden, and spring back when lightly pressed in the centre with your finger. If baking in batches, turn the cakes out onto a wire rack, then re-line the tins (careful not to burn yourself!) with new baking parchment and fill with the remaining coloured mixtures and bake as above. Set aside to cool completely.

continued overleaf

BAKE
IT
OFF

6 Make the buttercream by whisking the butter and icing sugar together using an electric hand mixer or stand mixer, until pale and fluffy. Add the food colouring of your choice and mix again briefly, until it's the colour you want.

7 Use a serrated knife to level the tops of the cakes. Place the violet-coloured cake on a cake board or plate, then slather the top with a generous amount of buttercream (around 5mm/¼in). Sandwich the indigo-coloured cake on top and slather this with buttercream too. Repeat with the blue, green, yellow, orange and red cakes, in that order.

8 Use a palette knife to spread a third of the remaining buttercream all over the cake in a thin layer – it's fine if the cake is still showing through; this is called a 'crumb coat' and will help to make the final buttercream layer neater.

9 Refrigerate the cake for 30 minutes, then spread half the remaining buttercream thickly over this layer, using a palette knife or frosting spatula to smooth it as much as possible. Add a little more food colouring to the remaining buttercream, if you like, then pipe in small rosettes around the top and bottom of the cake.

10 Decorate with your chosen friendship bracelet décor, if using: roll the white fondant into small balls, then flatten them slightly between your finger and thumb. These are your letters. Use black edible ink pen to write your chosen letters onto each piece, then arrange in a message on the top or side of the cake. Use coloured edible beads to build the rest of the bracelets.

Cruel summer pudding

There'll be no blue feelings while eating this pudding – only blue berries. While it looks like a pie, it's actually made by simply lining a pudding basin with stale bread and filling it with juicy berries that seep into the bread – a relic of times gone by, when cooks were more circumspect about letting nothing go to waste. Slicing into it is like cutting summer to the bone – a beautiful mass of blood-red, sweet–tart juices. For whatever it's worth, I've added a whisper of elderflower for the sunniest-sounding pudding you've ever heard.

SERVES 6

Equipment: 1 litre (1 quart) pudding basin

♥ VG

175g caster sugar
2 tbsp elderflower cordial
500g mixed berries (fresh or frozen – no strawberries, though, as they're too watery)
280g blueberries (fresh or frozen)
8 slices of stale white bread
Double cream, to serve

1. Line your pudding basin with cling film, making sure it hangs well over the edges.
2. Put the sugar and cordial in a large saucepan and bring slowly to the boil, stirring to dissolve the sugar. Add all the berries and cook over a medium heat, stirring, for 2–3 minutes (5–6 if using frozen berries), until the berries have just started to soften and release juice. Set aside to cool slightly.
3. Cut the crusts off all the slices of bread. Place one bread square in the bottom of the pudding basin. Now cut five of the bread slices at an angle across the middle, so you end up with wonky rectangles that are shorter at one end than the other. Place these, short side facing the bottom of the basin, along the sides of the basin, overlapping slightly. Cut the remaining two slices of bread in half from corner to corner, so you have two triangles.
4. Using a slotted spoon, take the fruit from the pan and place it into the lined basin, leaving the juice in the pan. Pour 4 tablespoons of the juice over the fruit. Put the remaining juice in a small bowl and chill in the fridge, for serving.
5. Place the bread triangles over the top of the pudding, longest sides facing outwards (so the points meet in the middle and you have a square).
6. Place another sheet of cling film over the top of the pudding, then find a plate that will sit exactly inside the pudding basin. Put it on the top of the cling film, then weigh it down (with, for example, a heavy can) and place in the fridge for at least 6 hours.
7. To serve, turn out the pudding onto a large plate or bowl. Serve the remaining berry juice alongside with some cold double cream.

Christmas tree farm cake

Amid stressful winter nights, I think we all want to escape to a Christmas tree farm in our hearts. With this cake, you can indulge all those sweet dreams of holly and ribbon and feed a crowd snuggled up in their winter warmers. It's simpler than it looks. You can buy readymade Christmas tree cake toppers if you don't want to make your own fondant trees. Serve in thick slices, let the cider flow and I hope all your Christmas wishes come true.

SERVES 10–12

Equipment: 25cm (10in) heart-shaped cake tin, an electric stand mixer or electric hand whisk, food processor

For the cake:
350g soft butter, plus extra for greasing the tin
350g caster sugar
½ tsp flaky salt
6 eggs, beaten
2 tsp vanilla extract
360g sifted plain flour
4 tsp baking powder

For the buttercream:
220g soft butter
375g sifted icing sugar

To decorate:
225g berry jam (use your favourite – I like raspberry)
4 x 114g packets of chocolate finger biscuits
154g packet of Oreo biscuits
225g green fondant icing
Silver lustre, for dusting
Icing sugar, for dusting

1 Preheat the oven to 170°C fan/190°C/375°F/gas 5. Grease the base and sides of your cake tin and line with baking parchment.

2 Beat the butter, sugar and salt using a stand mixer or an electric hand whisk until light and fluffy – about 3–5 minutes. Gradually add the eggs, whisking well between each addition. Once the eggs are all whisked in, add the vanilla, flour and baking powder and mix just enough to combine.

3 Pour the mixture into the prepared tin and level the top. Bake for 50 minutes–1 hour, until the cake is risen and golden and springs back when gently pressed with a finger. Set aside for 15 minutes to cool slightly, then remove from the tin and leave to cool completely on a wire rack.

4 Make the buttercream by whisking the butter and icing sugar together using a stand mixer or an electric hand mixer, until pale and well combined.

5 Once the cake has cooled completely, remove it from the tin and cut it in half horizontally with a serrated knife. Spread the bottom half of the cake thickly with the jam, then sandwich the other half on top.

6 Using a palette knife, cover the top and sides of the cake in a smooth layer of the buttercream. Arrange the chocolate fingers, pointing vertically, around the sides of the cake to form a fence – press them into the buttercream to stick them next to each other.

continued overleaf

7 Take the Oreo cookies and break them in half, scraping off the white filling so that you're left with just the black cookies. Place these in a food processor and blitz to fine crumbs, then scatter these crumbs in an even layer of 'soil' over the top of the cake (inside the 'fence').

8 Divide the fondant into 13 lumps of varying sizes. Roll each lump into a cone shape then, using a small pair of scissors, snip all over the sides of the cones. Use the tip of the scissors to flick each snipped piece out slightly, to form the spikes of the trees (see photo). Once you've done all 13, arrange the trees on top of the chocolate soil. Finally, dust the trees and cake with silver lustre and icing sugar, to finish.

It's nice to have a friand

Friands are delightfully moist little cakes made with butter and ground nuts, usually almonds. I make mine with coconut and they taste like old-fashioned macaroons or coconut ice – a nostalgia trip in one mouthful. Strawberries and coconut go beautifully together, and here they merge into beautifully pastel-pink little cakes that conjure up girlhood and good times. Why not share a nice friand with your nicest friends?

MAKES 12

Equipment: 12-hole cupcake tin
★ GF: swap the plain flour for gluten-free flour

For the cakes:
100g butter, melted and cooled slightly
4 egg whites
130g caster sugar
110g desiccated coconut
A pinch of salt
½ tsp vanilla extract
70g plain flour
6 strawberries

For the icing:
60g icing sugar
2–3 drops pink food colouring
3 tbsp sprinkles

1 Preheat the oven to 180°C fan/200°C/400°F/gas 6. Brush the insides of the cupcake tin with some of the melted butter and set aside the rest of the butter.

2 In a large bowl, whisk the egg whites until slightly frothy – no need to go too far; this isn't meringue. Whisk in the sugar, coconut, salt, vanilla and flour. The mixture will be quite stiff. Then, slowly pour in the melted butter, whisking as you go, to make a smooth batter.

3 Divide the batter between the holes in the cupcake tin (I use a mini ladle for this). Slice each strawberry in half, then place one half onto each cake, cut side facing upwards.

4 Bake for 20–30 minutes, until the cakes have risen and turned light golden around the edges. They should spring back when pressed with a finger. Leave to cool completely on a wire rack.

5 Make the icing. Sift the icing sugar into a medium bowl, then whisk in enough water – about ½–1 tbsp – and food colouring to create a light pink mixture the thickness of pancake batter. Drizzle the icing over the cooled cakes and scatter over the sprinkles.

photographed overleaf

Miss Americana and the Heartbreak Linzertortes

Linzertorte is an Austrian speciality from the city of Linz. It features a crumbly hazelnut pastry around a jam filling, similar to an Italian crostata or an old-fashioned jam tart. Come home and make this version – everyone will be whispering about what a good good baker you are. I make half of these with blue(berry) jam and half with red, in a nod to the divided scoreboard of 'Miss Americana and the Heartbreak Prince'!

MAKES 8

Equipment: food processor (optional), 8 mini tart tins 10cm (4in) in diameter, ideally with removable bases, baking beans, small heart-shaped cookie cutter

175g plain flour, plus extra for rolling the dough
80g ground hazelnuts (buy pre-ground or grind in a food processor)
50g icing sugar, sifted, plus extra for dusting
¼ tsp ground cinnamon
¼ tsp ground nutmeg
A pinch of ground cloves
Zest of 1 lemon
110g cold butter, cut into cubes
½ tsp flaky salt
2 egg yolks
8 tsp fresh breadcrumbs
140g blueberry jam
140g red jam (strawberry, raspberry or cherry)

1. Put the flour, hazelnuts, icing sugar, spices, lemon zest, butter and salt in a large bowl or food processor. Pulse (if using the food processor) or rub (if using your fingertips) everything together until the mixture resembles fine breadcrumbs. Add the egg yolks and bring the dough together, adding 1 tablespoon of water if it still feels too dry. Shape into a flat disc, then wrap in cling film and chill for 30 minutes.
2. On a lightly floured work surface, roll the dough to a thickness of around 3mm (⅛in). Using a cookie cutter or the rim of a bowl, cut into circles approximately 4cm (1½in) wider in diameter than your tart tins, then press the dough gently into the tart tins, ensuring there are no cracks or gaps. Prick the base of each pastry case with a fork, then chill for 15 minutes. Gather the remaining pastry together then wrap in cling film and place in the fridge too.
3. Preheat the oven to 190°C fan/210°C/400°F/gas 6. Line the pastry cases with squares of baking parchment and fill with baking beans. Set them on a baking tray and bake for 10 minutes, then remove the beans and pastry and bake for another 5 minutes.
4. Scatter a teaspoon of the breadcrumbs over the base of each cooked pastry case. Divide the blueberry jam between half of the tart cases, and the red jam between the remaining cases.
5. Roll out the remaining pastry on a lightly floured work surface and cut out heart shapes. Place these gently on top of each tart. Lower the oven temperature to 180°C fan/200°C/400°F/gas 6, then bake for 20 minutes, until the hearts are golden brown and the jam is bubbling. Remove from the oven and leave to cool completely before dusting with icing sugar and serving.

folklore

We're doing good, we're on some new treats. Been saying yes to time spent in the folklorian woods, where golden magic hovers around every corner. Moss clings to the gnarled contours of ancient tree bark, and tangled weeds hide ferocious, unbridled screams. Where peace is a hoax, but love stories are passed down like folk songs. It's a place of marvellous times, of epiphanies, of exile, of tears and of trying. Grab your cosiest cardigan and head into the forest, whose stories await.

Green was the grass where our heroine once read in Centennial Park, and it's also the colour of a pie so verdant, it might have walked out of the woods itself. When August slips away, it's a moment for betty – the brown, buttery variety that would be welcome to show up at anyone's party. Make a tart so beautiful you'll feel like it's shining just for you, or steal out to create some illicit éclairs that'll leave you flushed when you return. If it's an epiphany you're looking for, you might find it in a lacquered pastry pie heady with almond cream. If none of this feels like your homeland anymore, though, seek comfort in the familiar: a plate of crisp, buttery chai cookies.

illicit éclairs - key lime green pie - pear and apple brown betty

epiphany cake - this is me chai-ing cookies - i'm a mirabelle

illicit éclairs

You'll be flushed once you've had a bite of these beauties. The high might eventually dwindle, but it'll still be an éclair to remember. In the spirit of treacherous romance, these are packed full of ingredients said to have aphrodisiac properties: dark chocolate, figs and pomegranates. Don't be scared of making your own choux pastry – it's easier than it sounds and the results are infinitely better than anything you can buy. Serve these preferably in a beautiful room, but a parking lot will also do.

MAKES 10

Equipment: piping bag and nozzle, cocktail stick

For the choux pastry:
60g sifted plain flour
1 tsp caster sugar
55g butter
150ml cold water
2 eggs, beaten

For the filling and topping:
2 egg yolks
50g golden caster sugar
½ tsp vanilla paste
13g cornflour
200ml whole milk
5 figs, thinly sliced
100g dark chocolate
5 tbsp pomegranate seeds, to decorate
Icing sugar, for dusting (optional)

1 Preheat the oven to 200°C fan/220°C/425°F/gas 7. Line a baking tray with baking parchment or a non-stick liner. Place an empty baking tray at the bottom of the oven.

2 Make the pastry. Fold a sheet of baking parchment in half and then open it up again, so you have a crease down the centre. Put the sifted flour and caster sugar on top of the paper crease and set aside (this will enable you to 'shoot' the flour into the pan later).

3 Put the butter and water into a medium saucepan and bring to the boil, stirring to melt the butter. As soon as the mixture has come to the boil, turn off the heat and immediately 'shoot' the flour and sugar into the pan with one hand using the paper as a chute, while whisking vigorously with the other hand. Keep whisking until you have a smooth ball of paste that comes away cleanly from the sides of the pan – this will take around a minute.

4 Now add the beaten eggs, a little at a time, to the mixture in the pan, whisking vigorously between each addition. Once all the egg is added, keep whisking until you have a smooth, glossy paste.

5 Transfer the dough to a piping bag and pipe ten thick lines, each around 10cm (4in) long and 3cm (1¼in) wide, on the lined baking tray. Put the tray into the oven and quickly pour a jug of water into the baking tray you had placed at the bottom of the oven, to create steam.

continued overleaf

6 Bake for 20–25 minutes, until the pastry is golden brown and crispy. Remove from the oven and pierce the side of each éclair with a cocktail stick to let out the steam, then transfer to a wire rack and leave to cool completely. Once cool, slice them in half horizontally.

7 Make the crème pâtissière. Put the egg yolks, caster sugar, vanilla and cornflour in a small saucepan and whisk well. Add the milk, whisking as you go, then heat the mixture over a medium heat, whisking constantly. Continue to cook, whisking, until the mixture thickens so you can see the indentations made by the whisk – this will take 5–10 minutes. Don't heat it too high, or it will scramble. Once thick, pour the mixture into a bowl and cover with cling film. Set aside to cool.

8 Pipe the crème pâtissière along the bottom half of each éclair (or spread with a spoon if you don't have a piping bag). Top with the fig slices, then sandwich the top back on. Repeat for each éclair.

9 Melt the chocolate in a large heatproof bowl set over a pan of simmering water (don't let the bottom of the bowl touch the water). Spread the melted chocolate over the top of each éclair, then sprinkle with pomegranate seeds. Once the chocolate has set, dust with icing sugar before serving.

key lime green pie

I had a marvellous time playing around with the traditional key lime pie recipe here, and I hope I haven't ruined everything. A twist of makrut lime leaf gives an extra dimension to the citrus, while brown butter makes the crust even more delicious. I hope that Rebekah Harkness, a woman known for breaking the mould, would approve. You can buy frozen lime leaves in Asian groceries and makrut lime powder online, but leave it out if you can't find it, or use matcha instead. Fresh basil works wonderfully with lime and amps up the green – good for a pie, less good for dyeing the neighbour's dog. So choose the pie.

SERVES 8

Equipment: food processor, 23cm (9in) loose-bottomed tart tin, electric hand whisk, piping bag and nozzle
★ GF: use gluten-free biscuits for the pie crust

For the crust:
300g Hobnob, digestive or ginger nut biscuits
10 fresh or frozen makrut lime leaves
110g butter

For the filling:
4 egg yolks
Zest and juice of 4–5 limes (about 150ml)
½ tsp flaky salt
3 tsp makrut lime powder (optional)
400g can condensed milk

To serve:
150ml double cream
5g fresh basil leaves (the smaller leaves, if possible)

1 Preheat the oven to 170°C fan/190°C/375°F/gas 5. Put the biscuits and lime leaves in a food processor and blitz to fine crumbs. Set aside.

2 Put the butter in a medium saucepan and cook over a medium-high heat, swirling occasionally, until it is bubbling. Watch it closely during this time and don't let it burn – as soon as it starts to have brown flecks in it, turn off the heat. Add the biscuit crumbs to the butter and mix well.

3 Tip the crumbs into your tart tin and use the back of a spoon to press them all over the base and up the sides of the tin to form an even crust. Bake for 10 minutes, then remove and leave to cool.

4 Whisk the egg yolks and lime zest using an electric mixer or by hand, until paler and more voluminous. Add the salt and lime powder (if using) and whisk again briefly. Add the condensed milk and whisk again for 2–3 minutes, then add the lime juice and whisk again. Taste and adjust – you may want a little more lime juice or salt.

5 Once the tart case has cooled, pour the filling into it and spread it out with a spatula to even it out. Place the tart in the fridge and chill for at least 2 hours before serving.

6 To serve, whip the cream with an electric hand whisk to soft peaks. Transfer to a piping bag and pipe it in little rosettes around the edges of the tart. Place a couple of basil leaves on the top of each piped cream rosette.

photographed overleaf

pear and apple brown betty

They assumed she knew nothing, but Betty sure knew how to make a good dessert. A brown betty is a classic American dessert, with fruit baked under a crunchy topping made with buttery breadcrumbs. This one uses autumn fruit – apples and pears – since it's designed to be eaten once August has slipped away like a moment in time. Put on your cosiest cardigan, grab a spoon and enjoy. Leftovers are delicious for breakfast.

SERVES 4–6

Equipment: medium ovenproof frying pan

★ GF: use gluten-free breadcrumbs and oats

♥ VG: use a plant-based butter alternative

2 large Conference pears
1 cooking apple or 2 eating apples
110g butter
50g pecan nuts
4 tbsp maple syrup
50g light brown sugar
1 tsp ground cinnamon
½ tsp ground ginger
¼ tsp freshly grated nutmeg
70g soft breadcrumbs
70g rolled oats
Vanilla ice cream, to serve

1. Preheat the oven to 180°C fan/200°C/400°F/gas 6.
2. Cut the pears into quarters lengthways, and remove the cores. Slice them again into eighths. Peel and core the apple(s) and cut into thin slices.
3. Melt 30g of the butter in a medium ovenproof frying pan over a medium heat. Add the pears and cook them gently until lightly golden on all sides. Turn off the heat and scatter the apple pieces and pecan nuts among the pears. Drizzle over half the maple syrup.
4. While the pears are cooking, melt the remaining butter in a medium saucepan. Turn off the heat and stir in the brown sugar, cinnamon, ginger, nutmeg, breadcrumbs and oats. Mix well.
5. Tip the breadcrumb mixture evenly over the apples and pears in the pan. Drizzle over the remaining maple syrup.
6. Bake for 35 minutes, until the topping is golden and crispy. Serve with vanilla ice cream.

epiphany cake

If you're dreaming of some epiphany, you might just find it here. In France, Epiphany (6 January) is celebrated with galette des rois: king cake. Made from puff pastry encasing a luscious almond cream, it's often elaborately scored before baking for a beautiful intricate appearance. Many bakers add a dried broad bean to the mix – whoever finds it in their slice gets to be king for a day! However, it's less risky to the king's teeth to use a whole almond, as suggested here. I like to add a sharp berry jam to the almond filling to counterbalance the richness, but it's optional.

SERVES 6–8

80g ground almonds
80g golden caster sugar
Zest of 1 lemon
¼ tsp flaky salt
85g soft butter
2 tsp kirsch or amaretto (optional)
¼ tsp almond extract
3 eggs
400g pre-rolled puff pastry (either one rectangular piece or two circular pieces; if your pastry packet contains slightly more or less, that's fine – just make a slightly bigger or smaller tart)
100g raspberry or cherry jam (optional)
1 whole almond (optional)
1 tsp milk

1 In a medium bowl, mix together the almonds, sugar, lemon zest, salt, butter, kirsch (if using) and almond extract with a wooden spoon until soft and fluffy. Add two of the eggs and mix well until everything is combined. Place the bowl in the fridge while you prepare the pastry.

2 Preheat the oven to 190°C fan/210°C/400°F/gas 6. Line a large baking tray with baking parchment or a non-stick liner.

3 If your pastry is in a rectangle, cut it in half so you have two equal-sized squares. Cut circles from each square as large as possible, probably 20–23cm (8–9in) – the easiest way to do this is to cut around the base of a cake tin, but if you're doing it freehand, don't worry if your shapes end up a little oblong. Set aside any offcuts for decorating the tart. If you're using puff pastry circles, you're good to go.

4 Place one pastry circle on the lined baking tray. Smooth the almond cream evenly over it, leaving a border of 2.5cm (1in) all around the edge. If you're using the jam, smooth this as evenly as possible over the top of the almond cream (or drop it on top in teaspoonfuls if easier). If you're including the whole almond, place this somewhere on top of the filling.

continued overleaf

5 Brush the pastry border with a little water. Drape the other pastry circle over the top of the almond filling and press down around the border to seal it. Crimp together with your fingers – the best way to do this is to press down on the pastry border with the thumb and forefinger of one hand, fingers pointing away from the pastry, and use the forefinger of your other hand to press the pastry inwards between your two other fingers.

6 Using a sharp, pointed knife, score the pastry all over in a decorative pattern – the most traditional is simply curving lines from the centre out towards the edges. Be careful you don't cut through the pastry. Cut four small slits in the top (now you can cut through the pastry!), to allow steam to escape.

7 Beat the remaining egg with the milk and brush all over the surface of the pastry. Don't brush the crimped edges vertically, though, or it will stop the pastry rising properly. If you have any pastry offcuts, roll these out and cut into shapes, then place them on top of the pastry (avoiding the slits you've cut) and brush them with egg wash too.

8 Bake for 25–30 minutes, until the pastry is deep golden. Leave to cool completely before eating.

this is me chai-ing cookies

I just wanted you to know that this is me adapting my all-time favourite cookie recipe: Alison Roman's chocolate shortbread, so good it earned the nickname 'The Cookies' on social media. I've added warming chai spices as a nod to one of Taylor's favourite bakes. Use whatever chocolate chips you like: dark results in a less-sweet cookie, while milk or white work indulgently with the spices and give you the feeling you're enjoying a hot, sweet chai (which is definitely a better option than pouring the whisky). These will put the shine back in your wheels, for sure.

MAKES 20

Equipment: electric stand mixer or electric hand whisk

265g soft butter
100g granulated sugar
65g light brown sugar
1 tsp ground cinnamon
1 tsp ground ginger
¼ tsp ground cloves
¼ tsp ground allspice
½ tsp ground nutmeg
1 tsp ground cardamom
A pinch of chilli flakes
A couple of grinds of black pepper
¼ tsp flaky salt, plus extra for sprinkling
350g plain flour
240g chocolate chips of your choice
2 tbsp milk
2 tbsp demerara sugar

1. Place the butter, granulated sugar and light brown sugar in the bowl of an electric stand mixer or a large bowl. Beat well, using the mixer or an electric hand whisk, until the mixture is light and fluffy. Add the spices and salt along with the flour, then gently mix everything together to form a soft dough. Mix in the chocolate chips.
2. Shape the dough into a log around 5cm (2in) wide. Wrap in cling film and chill in the fridge for 2 hours.
3. Preheat the oven to 190°C fan/210°C/400°F/gas 6. Line two baking trays with baking parchment or non-stick liners.
4. Brush the cookie log all over with the milk, then scatter the demerara sugar over a plate and roll the log in it to coat it.
5. Slice the sugary cookie log into 1cm (⅜in)-wide pieces and lay each one flat on the baking trays. Sprinkle each cookie with a tiny pinch of salt.
6. Bake for 10–13 minutes, until the cookies are light golden brown and a little darker gold around the edges. Remove from the oven and leave to cool on a wire rack before eating.

i'm a mirabelle

This tart is shimmering beautiful. Mirabelles are small yellow plums, traditionally served in France in a tarte aux mirabelles. Once decorated with silver lustre and glitter, this tart looks remarkably like a mirrorball that'll show you all possible versions of yourself – or, actually, just the version that's really hungry for dessert. If you can't find mirabelles (which are in season in late summer), use any other plums, greengages or apricots – just try to get them as small as possible. The silky custard filling ensures the tart doesn't break into a million pieces – just try, try, try to resist the temptation of coming back for a second slice.

SERVES 6–8

Equipment: food processor, 23cm (9in) loose-bottomed tart tin, baking beans
★ GF: use shop-bought gluten-free pastry

For the pastry:
140g plain flour, plus extra for rolling the pastry
85g cold butter, cut into cubes
2 tbsp caster sugar
A pinch of salt
2–3 tbsp ice-cold water

For the filling:
680g mirabelle plums, or other small plums, halved and stones removed
100g caster sugar, plus 2 tbsp for the plums
2 tbsp cornflour
2 eggs
100ml whole milk
1 tsp vanilla paste
45ml double cream

For the decoration:
Edible silver lustre
Edible silver glitter

1 First make the pastry. Put all the ingredients except the water in a food processor and blitz until the mixture resembles breadcrumbs, or place them all into a bowl and rub the butter into the flour using your fingers. Add the water, a tablespoon at a time, until the dough just comes together, then tip out onto a work surface and bring together with your hands to a flat disc. Wrap in cling film and chill for 30 minutes.

2 Roll out the dough to a thickness of around 3mm (⅛in) on a floured work surface. Transfer to your tart tin and use to line it. There might be some overhang – you can trim this off after baking. Place the lined tin in the fridge for another 30 minutes. Preheat the oven to 180°C fan/200°C/400°F/gas 6.

3 Prick the pastry all over with a fork, then place a piece of baking parchment over it and fill with baking beans. Bake for 10 minutes, then remove the paper and beans and bake for another 8–10 minutes, until the pastry is a light golden brown. Remove and set aside. Turn the oven up to 200°C fan/220°C/425°F/gas 7.

4 Toss the plums in a bowl with the 2 tablespoons caster sugar and the cornflour. Place the eggs, 100g caster sugar, milk, vanilla and cream in a jug and whisk together well. Tip the plums into the pastry case, spreading them out as evenly as possible. Tip the milk mixture over the top.

5 Put the tart in the oven and bake for 40–45 minutes, until the pastry edges are a deep golden brown, the plums are slightly scorched and the custard has a slight wobble. Remove from the oven and leave to cool.

6 Dust the cooled tart with silver lustre and sprinkle with glitter before serving. Shimmering beautiful!

evermore

'Tis the damn season for silken fog shrouding windowpanes. Flushes and flannel. An autumn chill that wakes you up. It gets colder and colder, the sun going down, setting on suburban dreams. The year is slowly getting its closure.

Retreat in your mind to a creaky-floored cabin, a chilly mist hovering at the window. Turn on the oven, bring out the warming spices and cocoon yourself in a soothing blanket of sweetness. Even if you don't like a gold rush, you'll love a tender crumb softly scented with rose. If the holidays are lingering like cheap perfume, serve up a tangy frozen cheesecake to help you tolerate it, or cut a long story short with crumbly cookies out of a wild wonderland. Allow an ivy-covered cake to take root in your dreams with its heady combination of matcha and lime, or splash out on a bottle and indulge in some very unproblematic champagne macarons. Honour the fallen Este with a rich almond and caramel cake that'll have all your friends swearing they're with you, so they can have a slice.

You won't be fazed by a dull November when you've got these recipes up your sleeve.

long story shortbread

For days when it feels like you've fallen off the pedestal, pick yourself back up with these charmingly bookish cookies. They're a simple shortbread scented with Earl Grey, because I'm pretty sure that's what you get served at a tea party when you fall down the rabbit hole. You can decorate them in any way you like – perhaps with your favourite book titles. Grab some icing pens and get creative.

MAKES AROUND 15

Equipment: electric stand mixer or electric hand whisk, food processor, a book-shaped cookie cutter for this recipe (I got mine from Amazon)

♥ VG: use a plant-based butter alternative

65g golden caster sugar
3 tsp loose-leaf Earl Grey tea
A pinch of salt
125g soft butter
140g plain flour, plus extra for rolling the dough
35g rice flour
2 tbsp apricot jam
225g readymade white fondant icing
Icing sugar, for rolling the fondant
Fine edible writing pens, to decorate
Strong coffee, to decorate (optional)

1. Put the caster sugar and Earl Grey tea into a food processor and blitz until the tea is in fine dark speckles. Tip this into the bowl of an electric stand mixer, or a large bowl, and add the salt and butter. Beat with the mixer, an electric whisk, or a wooden spoon until pale and well combined, then add the flours. Bring everything together into a soft dough and wrap in cling film. Chill in the fridge for 30 minutes.
2. Preheat the oven to 150°C fan/170°C/340°F/gas 3. Line a large baking tray with baking parchment or a non-stick liner.
3. Roll out the dough on a floured work surface to around 5mm (¼in) thick. Use your cookie cutter to cut book shapes out of the dough, and place them on the lined baking tray, spaced slightly apart. Roll out any offcuts and cut again. Repeat until all the dough is used up.
4. Bake for 30 minutes, until lightly golden. Transfer to a wire rack and leave to cool completely.
5. Put the apricot jam in a small saucepan with 1 tablespoon water and bring to the boil. Cook for a minute, stirring, until you have a syrupy glaze. Remove from the heat.
6. Roll out the fondant icing on a worktop dusted with icing sugar to around 3mm (⅛in) thick. Use the same cookie cutter to cut out book shapes. Brush each cookie with the apricot jam, then layer a piece of fondant on top of each, pressing down gently.
7. Leave the fondant to dry out for around an hour. Then decorate with your chosen book titles or inscriptions using the edible writing pens. For an antique look, use a clean sponge to apply a little strong coffee to the page corners.

'tis the damson season

Write this down: this frozen damson creation looks real good now. It's somewhere between a parfait and a cheesecake: a buttery biscuit base topped with creamy vanilla rippled with tart damson purée, and served with the kind of chill that clouds your windshield glass. Perfect for the holidays, whether you're staying at your parents' house or not. Damsons are small, very sour plums – if you can't find them, use regular plums instead and halve the quantity of sugar in the purée.

SERVES 8

Equipment: 900g (2lb) loaf tin, food processor, an electric hand whisk

For the damson purée:
450g damsons or red plums (if using regular plums, quarter them and remove the stones)
100g caster sugar

For the biscuit base:
175g digestive biscuits
110g butter
½ tsp ground ginger

For the cheesecake cream:
300ml double cream
200g full-fat cream cheese
¼ tsp flaky salt
1 tsp vanilla paste
100g sifted icing sugar

1. Line the loaf tin with cling film.
2. Put the damsons or plums, sugar and 2 tablespoons water in a large saucepan and bring to the boil, stirring. Turn the heat down to medium, cover the pan, and let the plums bubble away for 10–15 minutes, until completely soft.
3. If using damsons, tip the mixture into a colander over a large bowl and use the back of a ladle to press as much purée through the holes in the colander as possible, until only the stones and a little pulp are left behind. If using plums, skip this step. Set aside the damson/plum mixture to cool completely.
4. Meanwhile, make the biscuit base. Blitz the biscuits to fine crumbs using a food processor. Melt the butter in a large saucepan, add the ginger and remove from the heat. Stir in the biscuit crumbs, mix well, and set aside.
5. Whip the double cream to soft peaks using an electric hand whisk, then add the cream cheese, salt, vanilla and icing sugar, and whisk again briefly until just combined.
6. Pour the plum mixture into the cheese mixture and mix gently with a large spoon. Don't mix it in completely – you want a ripple effect of pink through white.
7. Tip the mixture into the lined loaf tin. Scatter the biscuit mixture evenly over the top, pressing it down gently with the back of a spoon to form a fairly compact layer.
8. Place the tin in the freezer and chill for at least 6 hours before serving.
9. To serve, place a plate over the top of the tin, invert the cheesecake and release from the tin, then remove the cling film and cut into slices.

evermoorish lemon cake

If you're feeling down about a grey November, this citrus olive oil cake will put a spring back in your step. It's both moreish – the perfect balance of sweet and sour – and Moorish, inspired by the syrup cakes of North Africa, though my recipe is based on that of food writer Diana Henry. It's also evermore-ish, since it'll earn a firm place in your regular baking repertoire. Ideally, serve in a cabin where the floors creak under your step, windows open to the frost – or simply with a scoop of crème fraîche.

SERVES 8

Equipment: 20cm (8in) springform round cake tin, food processor
★ GF: use gluten-free bread and baking powder

For the cake:
150ml good-quality olive oil, plus extra for greasing the tin
60g stale white or sourdough bread (without crusts)
105g blanched almonds
1 tsp fresh lemon thyme leaves, or 2 tsp finely chopped fresh lemon verbena
Zest of 2 lemons
150g golden caster sugar
2 tsp baking powder
4 eggs, beaten
Icing sugar, for dusting
Candied lemon peel, to decorate (optional)

For the syrup:
100g caster sugar
50ml water
50ml lemon juice (from 2–3 lemons)

1. Preheat the oven to 170°C fan/190°C/375°F/gas 5. Grease the tin with a little of the olive oil and line the base with a circle of baking parchment.
2. Tear the bread into rough chunks and put it in a food processor with the almonds and thyme or verbena leaves, and the lemon zest. Blitz as finely as possible. Put this into a bowl and add the sugar, baking powder, olive oil and eggs. Whisk together until well combined.
3. Pour the mixture into the tin and bake for 35–45 minutes, until just set and a skewer inserted in the middle comes out clean.
4. Make the syrup by placing all the ingredients in a small saucepan and bringing to the boil, stirring to dissolve the sugar. Simmer for 5–10 minutes, until the mixture has reduced and thickened slightly.
5. Remove the cake from the oven and prick it all over with a skewer or cocktail stick, then drizzle your citrus syrup all over the cake, letting it sink into the holes.
6. Leave to cool before removing from the tin and dusting with icing sugar. Decorate with candied lemon peel.

ivy cake

The sight of this cake will bring a glow to your eyes. Plucked from the heart of the folklorian woods, it's earthy with grassy matcha and freshened by tangy lime curd. Covered in barely-there buttercream, it's a house of stone ensconced in snaking tendrils of (fondant) ivy leaves, edible flowers and fresh herbs, finished with a dusting of mossy matcha and stony silver. Drink your husband's wine, if you have one, and savour a little piece of nature while clover blooms in the fields.

SERVES 8–10

Equipment: three 15cm (6in) springform round cake tins, an electric stand mixer or electric hand whisk, cake turntable (optional, but useful)

For the cakes:
265g soft butter, plus extra for greasing
250g caster sugar
3 tbsp culinary matcha powder
½ tsp flaky salt
4 eggs, beaten
60g plain yoghurt
30ml milk
280g self-raising flour
¼ tsp baking powder

For the lime curd:
Zest and juice of 2 limes
75g caster sugar
45g butter
1 egg and 1 egg yolk

For the buttercream:
105g soft butter
185g sifted icing sugar

For the decoration:
100g green fondant icing
Edible fresh or dried flowers
Sprigs of fresh herbs
2 tsp matcha powder
2 tsp edible silver lustre

1 Preheat the oven to 170°C fan/190°C/375°F/gas 5. Grease and line the three cake tins.

2 Beat the butter and sugar using an electric stand mixer or electric hand whisk until light and fluffy – about 3–5 minutes. Add the matcha and salt and whisk briefly to mix. The batter should be a vivid jade green. Gradually add the eggs, whisking well between each addition. Once the eggs are all whisked in, add the yoghurt and milk and mix again. Finally, add the flour and baking powder and mix just enough to combine.

3 Divide the mixture between the three tins. Bake for 30–35 minutes, until the cakes are risen, golden and spring back when lightly pressed in the centre with your finger. Set aside to cool, then transfer to a wire rack to cool completely.

4 Meanwhile, make the lime curd. Put all the ingredients into a heatproof bowl set over a saucepan of simmering water over a medium heat (don't let the water touch the bottom of the bowl). Whisk continually – it will go a bit lumpy at first before the butter melts. Keep whisking for 5–10 minutes, until the curd thickens enough that you can see the traces of the whisk in it. Remove from the heat and set aside to cool – once it's at room temperature you can cover it and put it in the fridge (this can be done in advance).

5 Make the buttercream by whisking the butter and icing sugar together using an electric stand mixer or electric hand whisk, until pale and well combined.

continued overleaf

6 Use a serrated knife to level the tops of the cakes. Place one of the cakes on a cake board or plate, then slather the top with half of the lime curd. Sandwich another cake on top and slather this with the remaining lime curd. Set the final cake on top.

7 Use a palette knife to spread half the buttercream all over the cake in a thin layer – it's fine if the cake is still showing through; this is called a 'crumb coat'. Refrigerate the cake for 30 minutes to set the buttercream, then spread the remaining buttercream over the top of the first layer. It's fine if a little sponge still shows through – you want a 'naked cake' vibe.

8 Roll out the fondant to 3mm (⅛in) thick, then cut ivy leaves out of it with a sharp pointed knife (use a photo as a guide). It looks best if you make a few leaves of different sizes. Stick these to the sides of the cake, pressing them into the buttercream, then arrange your edible flowers and herbs over the cake. Finally, sift a little matcha and silver lustre over the top and sides of the cake.

champagne problemon macarons

Show those hometown sceptics who's boss with a plate of these melt-in-the-mouth macarons. They're bound to get your friends applauding. Macarons might seem intimidating to make, but they're actually quite simple – the key is to measure accurately, get the batter to the correct stage before piping and let them dry out slightly before baking. Subtly lemon-scented, these are packed with a toasty champagne-flavoured buttercream – but you can replace the champagne with a non-alcoholic sparkling wine if you like, or apple juice.

MAKES 15

Equipment: electric hand whisk, a piping bag with nozzle
★ GF

For the macarons:
100g granulated sugar
Zest of 1 lemon
100g egg whites (from 3 medium eggs)
⅛ tsp yellow food colouring paste
100g icing sugar, sifted
100g ground almonds
A pinch of salt
Edible gold lustre or glitter, to decorate

For the buttercream:
80ml champagne or sparkling wine
55g soft butter
120g icing sugar
A pinch of salt
1 tsp lemon juice

1 Put the granulated sugar and lemon zest in a small bowl and rub together with your fingertips for 1–2 minutes to release the fragrant oils.

2 Bring a small saucepan of water to the boil, then turn off the heat. Set a heatproof bowl on top of the pan, making sure the bottom of the bowl doesn't touch the water. Put the egg whites and 3 tablespoons of the lemony granulated sugar into this bowl. Using an electric whisk, whisk together for 1–2 minutes, until frothy and the sugar has completely dissolved. The mixture should not be at all grainy.

3 Remove the bowl from the pan of water and place on the worktop. Whisk the egg whites and sugar again until the mixture stands up in soft peaks when you remove the whisk. Now add the remaining lemony sugar, a little at a time, as you whisk, and enough food colouring to make it pale yellow. You should now have a stiff meringue mixture.

4 Sift the icing sugar, ground almonds and salt into the bowl of egg whites and sugar. Whisk for 5 seconds so that everything is just combined.

5 Using a large metal spoon, mix everything in the bowl using a folding motion – scoop the batter up from the outsides of the bowl and drop it in the centre, flicking your wrist in a clockwise circular motion. Once you can draw a heart shape with the batter that falls off the spoon without the line breaking as you draw, it's ready.

continued overleaf

6 Line two baking trays with baking parchment or non-stick liners. Pipe the batter onto the trays in small circles, around 4cm (1½in) in diameter. Leave them to dry out for 30–40 minutes, until the mixture feels almost dry and tacky to the touch. Do not skip this step!

7 Preheat the oven to 150°C fan/170°C/340°F/gas 3. Bake the macarons for 13–15 minutes, until lightly golden and firm but still slightly springy. Allow to cool completely.

8 For the buttercream, pour the champagne into a small saucepan and bring to the boil. Cook over a medium heat for 3–5 minutes, until reduced to 2 tablespoons. Leave to cool completely.

9 Put the butter, icing sugar and salt into a medium bowl and beat together with an electric whisk for 2–3 minutes, until well combined. Add the reduced champagne and lemon juice, then beat briefly again to combine.

10 Place the buttercream into a piping bag. Flip half the macarons over, so the underside is facing up, and pipe a spiral of buttercream onto these, around 5mm (¼in) high. Sandwich the remaining macarons on top.

11 Dust the macarons with edible gold lustre or glitter. Keep chilled until needed, then remove from the fridge around 30 minutes before serving.

gold rush financiers

Anticipating these might have you in a red flush. Not only are they covered in edible gold, but financiers – buttery almond cakes, originally from France – are so-called because the moulds they are made in resemble gold ingots. This is a gold rush you will like – there's richness in every bite, and a delicate hint of rose blush. Take them to a dinner party to distract from any contrarian personalities, and serve with a cup of fresh – not day-old – tea.

MAKES 12

Equipment: a 12-hole silicone financier mould, an electric hand whisk
★ GF: replace the plain flour with gluten-free flour

125g butter, melted and cooled slightly
4 egg whites
130g caster sugar
120g ground almonds
A pinch of salt
1½ tbsp rose water
45g plain flour

To decorate:
Edible gold lustre
Dried edible rose petals or rosebuds
Edible gold leaf (optional)

1 Preheat the oven to 180°C fan/200°C/400°F/gas 6. Brush the insides of the financier mould with some of the melted butter and set the rest of the butter aside.

2 In a large bowl, whisk the egg whites with an electric hand whisk until slightly frothy – no need to go too far; this isn't meringue. Whisk in the sugar, almonds, salt, rose water and flour. The mixture will be quite stiff. Then, slowly pour in the melted butter, whisking as you go, to incorporate it and create a smooth batter.

3 Divide the batter between the holes in the financier mould (I use a mini ladle for this).

4 Bake for 20–25 minutes, until the cakes have risen and turned light golden. They should spring back when pressed with a finger.

5 Transfer to a wire rack and leave to cool completely before dusting with edible gold lustre and decorating with edible rose petals or rosebuds. A few delicate pieces of edible gold leaf look good too.

photographed overleaf

no body no Daim cake

Daim cake is a Swedish classic, inspired by the Daim chocolate bar. The original is quite tricky to make, so I've simplified it here: a rich almond sponge, sandwiched with caramel buttercream and covered in melted Daim chocolate. If you can't find Daim bars or Daim chocolate, simply mix chopped almonds into melted milk chocolate for the topping. No bodies were harmed in the creation of this recipe, but it does taste so good that it's almost a crime.

SERVES 8

Equipment: 20cm (8in) springform round cake tin, an electric stand mixer or electric hand whisk

★ GF: use gluten-free flour and baking powder

For the cake:
195g soft butter
200g golden caster sugar
4 eggs, beaten
1 tsp almond extract
150g ground almonds
45g plain or gluten-free flour
½ tsp baking powder

For the caramel buttercream:
100g caster sugar
100ml double cream
½ tsp flaky salt
70g soft butter
125g icing sugar, sifted

For the topping:
225g Cadbury's Dairy Milk with Daim bar chocolate or 200g dark chocolate, plus 1 chopped Daim bar

1. Preheat the oven to 160°C fan/180°C/350°F/gas 4. Grease your cake tin and line with baking parchment.
2. Using an electric stand mixer or electric hand whisk, cream the butter and sugar together for 3–5 minutes, until light and fluffy. Add the eggs, a little at a time, whisking well between each addition. Add the almond extract, ground almonds, flour and baking powder, and mix gently until just combined.
3. Tip the batter into the prepared tin and bake for 50 minutes, until risen and golden and the centre springs back when pressed lightly with a finger. Transfer to a wire rack to cool completely.
4. Make the caramel for the buttercream. Put the caster sugar in a medium saucepan over a high heat. The sugar will begin to melt at the edges – swirl the pan to help it melt evenly, but do not stir. Once all the sugar has melted and started to turn golden, lower the heat to medium and cook for another 30 seconds or so, until you have a deep golden caramel. Immediately turn off the heat. Whisk in the double cream and salt, and set aside to cool.
5. Make the buttercream by whisking the butter and icing sugar together using an electric stand mixer or electric hand whisk, until pale and well combined. Pour in the cooled caramel and whisk briefly to combine.
6. Once the cake is completely cool, slice in half horizontally. Sandwich the two halves together with the caramel buttercream.
7. Melt the Daim chocolate in a heatproof bowl set over a pan of simmering water (don't let the water touch the bottom of the bowl). Leave to cool for 5 minutes, then spread over the top of the cake. Leave to set for 30–60 minutes before eating.

Midnights

Diamonds sparkling in jewel-bright eyes. The gentle perfume of lavender. Midnight rain blurring the aurora borealis. Falling in love as the plane turns right around. A gentle breeze in your hair. Romance is not dead if you make it yours, and what better love language than cake?

Your kitchen is going to be bejeweled once you're done with this era, Dear Reader. You certainly won't be the problem if you're bringing any of these Midnights-inspired concoctions to a dinner party; at tea time, everybody will agree that you're a baker who deserves the penthouse of anyone's heart. Whip up lavender haze cookies that you won't want to get off your desk (or countertop), or leave a real legacy with a deep Maroon velvet cake. Make it snow with showers of coconut, or avoid ending up on the floor by putting your roommate's rosé into a dessert instead of your wine glass.

Once you've survived the great war, clean up the kitchen and relax like a contented cat with a batch of good karma cat cookies.

Karma is a cat cookies

These cookies aren't just sweet like honey; they are deliciously honeyed. They're based on a Danish Christmas cookie recipe. Making these should be a relaxing thought – they come together very easily, and everything is made in one pan. Flex your skills like an acrobat and present the cat lady in your life with a batch of these for some very good karma indeed. Benjamin, Olivia and Meredith would approve.

MAKES AROUND 20, DEPENDING ON YOUR CUTTER

Equipment: cat-shaped cookie cutter

120g flavoursome honey, such as buckwheat or heather
100g dark brown sugar
110g butter
½ tsp bicarbonate of soda
½ tsp baking powder
1 egg
1 tsp vanilla extract
300g plain flour, plus extra for rolling the dough

To decorate:
Black edible icing pen
Edible gold lustre or glitter

1 Put the honey, sugar and butter into a large saucepan and melt together over a medium heat. Turn off the heat and immediately add the bicarbonate of soda and baking powder. The mixture will foam up and then subside. Once it does, beat in the egg and vanilla, then mix in the flour until just combined. You should have a soft dough. Put in a bowl and chill in the fridge for 1 hour.

2 Preheat the oven to 180°C fan/200°C/400°F/gas 6. Line two baking trays with baking parchment or a non-stick liner.

3 Roll the dough out on a floured work surface to around 6mm (¼in) thick. Use your cookie cutter to cut out shapes, then place them on the prepared baking trays, a little apart. Gather up any remaining dough and roll out again, until it is all used up.

4 Bake the cookies for 10–12 minutes, until they are a few shades darker. Transfer to a wire rack to cool before drawing on faces in black writing icing and dusting with edible gold lustre or glitter.

Maroon velvet cake

When morning comes, you'll be sneaking back to the counter for another slice of this cake, like it's your best friend. It's an ode to burgundy and blushing, carnations and roses, and you'll leave quite the legacy if you ever take it to a dinner party. You should use food colouring paste here rather than a liquid colouring, as it results in a deeper colour.

SERVES 10–12

Equipment: two 20cm (8in) springform round cake tins, an electric stand mixer or electric hand whisk, piping bag and nozzle, cake turntable and frosting spatula (optional, but useful)

For the cakes:
150ml vegetable oil, plus extra for greasing
280g plain flour
1½ tbsp cocoa powder
2 tsp baking powder
1 tsp bicarbonate of soda
½ tsp salt
250g light brown sugar
2 eggs
120g plain yoghurt
60ml whole milk
2 tsp vanilla extract
¼–½ tsp red food colouring paste

For the frosting and decoration:
110g soft butter
280g icing sugar
200g full-fat cream cheese
1 tsp vanilla paste
A pinch of salt
3 tbsp freeze-dried raspberries (optional)

1. Preheat the oven to 170°C fan/190°C/375°F/gas 5. Grease the two cake tins and line with baking parchment.
2. In a large bowl, whisk together the flour, cocoa, baking powder, bicarbonate of soda, salt and sugar.
3. In a large jug, whisk together the eggs, oil, yoghurt, milk, vanilla and enough food colouring to turn the mixture a deep red. Pour this into the dry ingredients.
4. Whisk everything together gently until you have a smooth batter – don't overmix. It should be a deep red – if it looks too pale, whisk in a little more food colouring.
5. Divide the batter between the two cake tins and bake for 25–30 minutes, until risen and the tops spring back when pressed lightly with a finger. Set aside to cool completely.
6. For the frosting, beat the butter and icing sugar together in a large bowl using an electric stand mixer or electric hand whisk, until pale and well combined. Add the cream cheese, vanilla and salt and whisk to mix thoroughly.
7. Use a spatula to spread the top of one of the cakes thickly (a layer of around 1cm/½in) with the cream cheese frosting, then sandwich the other cake on top. Cover the whole cake in a thin layer of the frosting, making sure you get a lot of it into the join between the two cakes so that the side of the cake looks even all around. Don't worry if there is still some cake showing through the frosting – you'll do another coat. Chill the cake for 30 minutes.

continued overleaf

8 Give the cake another layer of frosting, this time a little thicker, so you can't see any cake through the frosting anymore. You should still have a little frosting left – transfer it to a piping bag and use this to pipe small rosettes around the edge of the top of the cake.

9 To decorate the cake, if you like, make a stencil using baking parchment, cutting out shapes like those in the photograph on the previous page. Place it gently over the middle of the cake. Using a pestle and mortar, crush the dried raspberries into a fine powder. With a teaspoon, dust this into each hole of the stencil, then gently peel away the paper. Or you could simply dust around the edges of the cake with the raspberry powder.

Snow on the beach coconut passionfruit layer cake

One night, some time ago, I dreamed up this cake. It's covered in snowy coconut and tastes like a tropical beach, thanks to the passionfruit filling. The delicate coconut sponge is based on a recipe by one of my favourite bakers, Dan Lepard, and is beautifully moist and creamy, while the lime stops all the flavours from cloying. Once you've made and assembled the cake, you'll have a winning smile, for sure. Be proud of yourself, pour yourself a coconut rum and tuck in.

SERVES 10

Equipment: three 20cm (8in) springform round cake tins, an electric stand mixer or electric hand whisk

For the cake:
150ml full-fat coconut milk
50g desiccated coconut
1 tsp vanilla extract
Zest of 2 limes
A pinch of salt
250g butter, at room temperature, plus extra for greasing the tins
250g caster sugar
3 eggs, beaten
280g plain flour
2 tsp baking powder
3 tbsp white or coconut rum (optional)

For the buttercream:
280g soft butter
500g icing sugar, sifted
Zest of 2 limes and 2 tsp juice

To assemble and decorate:
4 tbsp shop-bought passionfruit coulis, or the pulp of 4 passionfruit
50g desiccated or 50g flaked coconut
½ ripe mango, peeled

1 Put the coconut milk in a small saucepan and bring to the boil. Remove from the heat and add the desiccated coconut, vanilla, lime zest and salt. Stir and set aside.

2 Preheat the oven to 160°C fan/180°C/350°F/gas 4. Grease your cake tins and line with baking parchment.

3 Using an electric stand mixer or electric hand whisk, beat the butter and sugar together for 3–5 minutes, until light and fluffy. Gradually add the eggs, a little at a time, beating well between each addition. Gently mix in the plain flour, baking powder and the coconut milk mixture until you have a smooth batter.

4 Divide the batter between the three tins, then bake for 30–35 minutes, until golden and risen, and the sponges spring back when gently pressed with a finger. While they are still warm, brush the top of each sponge with the rum (if using). Leave to cool for 10 minutes, then remove from the tins and leave to cool completely on a wire rack.

5 Make the buttercream. Put all the ingredients in a large bowl and beat using an electric stand mixer or electric hand whisk until light and fluffy.

continued overleaf

6 Once the cakes are cool, level the tops with a serrated knife held horizontally. Spread the top of two of the sponges with a thin layer of buttercream, then spread half the passionfruit on each of those sponges – don't spread it right to the edge, or it might leak out when the cakes are stacked. Stack the three sponges on top of each other, the plain one on top.

7 Using a palette knife, spread the buttercream all over the stack of sponges, working it into any gaps around the sides so you have an even layer, and over the top. Using your hands, press the desiccated or flaked coconut onto the buttercream to completely cover the cake.

8 Slice the mango into wedges. Use the wedges to create a palm tree shape on top of the cake (see photo).

Lavender haze hearts

This is really two recipes in one. The first is a fragrant sugar that can liven up all manner of dishes – try sprinkling it over meringues. The second combines this sugar with butter (you can substitute with a vegan alternative) and flour for a crisp yet tender shortbread with the subtle fragrance of lavender. You'll handle it beautifully. These will send you into a dizzying love spiral – you won't find it hard to get them off your desk.

MAKES AROUND 13

Equipment: food processor, an electric stand mixer, heart-shaped cookie cutters

♥ VG: use a plant-based butter alternative

For the lavender sugar:
100g caster sugar
4 tbsp dried lavender buds (make sure your lavender is for culinary use)

For the cookies:
110g soft butter
65g lavender sugar (see above), plus extra for sprinkling
A pinch of salt
130g plain flour, plus extra for rolling out the dough
45g rice flour
Lavender sprigs, to decorate
Edible purple glitter or lustre, for dusting

1. For the sugar, place the sugar and lavender in a food processor and blitz until well combined and very fragrant.
2. Using an electric stand mixer – or a wooden spoon – beat the butter in a large bowl until soft and creamy. Add 65g of the lavender sugar and salt and beat well to combine. Sift in the flours, then mix to a soft dough. Wrap the dough in baking parchment and place in the fridge for 30 minutes to firm up.
3. Roll the dough out on a floured surface to 1cm (½in) thick. Using a heart-shaped cookie cutter or a sharp knife, cut the dough into heart shapes. Arrange on a piece of baking parchment or a silicone non-stick liner on a baking tray. Press a lavender sprig into each cookie, then place in the fridge for 15 minutes to firm up.
4. Preheat the oven to 150°C fan/170°C/340°F/gas 3.
5. Bake the cookies for 25–30 minutes (depending on what size you made them), until light golden brown. Remove from the oven and sprinkle with a little of the remaining lavender sugar. Leave to cool completely before dusting with purple edible glitter or lustre.

Rosé poached pears cake

Best not to end up on the floor, so put your rosé into this cake instead (maybe don't use your roommate's). Use it to poach pears into translucent lusciousness, then ensconce them in a delicious, cardamom-scented almond batter. The result is an easy but impressive-looking cake ideal for serving as a dinner party dessert with a scoop of crème fraîche. You can use a budget rosé (screw top optional), but it's better to use one that you'd actually drink – then you can enjoy the rest of the bottle while you prepare this recipe.

SERVES 8

Equipment: 900g (2lb) loaf tin, an electric stand mixer or electric hand whisk

For the pears:
480ml rosé wine
150g caster sugar
1 vanilla pod, split lengthways
A strip of lemon peel
A strip of orange peel
2 bay leaves (fresh or dried)
3 medium pears (Comice or Conference are best) – enough to fit snugly upright in your loaf tin

For the cake:
140g soft butter, plus extra for greasing
150g golden caster sugar
1 tsp vanilla extract
1 tsp ground cardamom
Zest of 1 lemon
2 eggs, beaten
90g plain flour
40g ground almonds
½ tsp baking powder
2 tbsp demerara sugar
Icing sugar, for dusting

1 Put the rosé and sugar into a medium saucepan and bring to the boil, stirring to dissolve the sugar. Add the vanilla pod, citrus peel and bay leaves, then lower the heat to a medium-low simmer. Peel the pears and use a sharp knife to cut the core out of the bottom. Place the pears in the wine, cover with a lid, and cook on a medium simmer for around 30 minutes, turning occasionally, until they are tender to the point of a knife. Remove the pears from the wine with a slotted spoon, drain on kitchen roll and set aside to cool.

2 Preheat the oven to 170°C fan/190°C/375°F/gas 5. Grease your loaf tin and line with baking parchment.

3 Put the butter and sugar in the bowl of an electric stand mixer or a large bowl. Beat together using the mixer or an electric whisk until pale and fluffy – around 3–5 minutes. Add the vanilla, cardamom and lemon zest, along with the eggs, a little at a time, until fully incorporated. Add the flour, ground almonds and baking powder, then mix until just combined.

4 Spoon a little of the cake batter into the loaf tin – a layer around 2.5cm (1in) thick. Arrange the pears, stalk side up, in one line in the loaf tin on top of this layer of batter. They should be snug next to each other.

5 Spoon the remaining cake batter around the pears – a little between each pear, and between the pears and the sides of the tin. Sprinkle the demerara sugar evenly over the top.

6 Bake for 45–60 minutes, until the cake springs back when lightly pressed with a finger, and/or a skewer inserted into the cake comes out clean. Leave to cool completely.

7 Dust with icing sugar, and serve.

Bejeweled cookies

The whole place will be shimmering once you've made these cookies. Grab your edible glitter and tell your friends that, by the way, you're staying in tonight. You could even get a selection of jewel-shaped cookie cutters to make a full-on jewel box that will polish up your next dinner party real nice.

MAKES AROUND 20

Equipment: jewel-shaped cookie cutter with an 'embossing' side, approximately 6cm (2½in). (I got mine from Birkmann)

For the cookies:
1 batch of the Foxes in boxes cookie dough (page 61), shaped into a flat disc and chilled for 1 hour
Plain flour, for rolling the dough
2 tbsp strawberry, raspberry or apricot jam
Icing sugar, for rolling the fondant
200g pink fondant icing
Edible glitter (blue, purple and silver work well together)

1 Preheat the oven to 190°C fan/210°C/400°F/gas 6. Line two baking trays with baking parchment or non-stick liners.

2 Roll out the cookie dough on a floured work surface to around 5mm (¼in) thick. Use the non-embossing side of the cookie cutter to cut out jewel shapes, then place on the prepared baking trays, at least 2.5cm (1in) apart. Shape any excess dough into a ball, roll out again and cut more jewels – repeat until it is all used up.

3 Bake for 10–12 minutes, until the cookies are golden brown. Transfer to a wire rack and leave to cool completely.

4 Mix the jam with 1 tablespoon of water in a small saucepan, then cook over a medium heat for 1–2 minutes, until bubbling and syrupy. Set aside.

5 Dust a work surface lightly with icing sugar and roll out the fondant to a thickness of around 3mm (⅛in). Use the non-embossing side of the cookie cutter to cut the jewel outline out of the fondant.

6 Brush each cookie with a little of the jam, then place a fondant jewel on top. Use the embossing side of the cookie cutter to press a jewel outline into the soft fondant, then repeat with the remaining cookies.

7 Once all the fondant is in place, brush each piece lightly with the jam, then dust with the edible glitter.

THE TORTURED POETS DEPARTMENT

How can you be guilty as sin for chanting MORE when you see what this era has to offer? Its lyricism is swirled into every one of these edible poems, but there's nothing tortured about these treats except their inspiration. There are enough ideas in here to fill a fortnight, and once they're fresh out the oven you'll be coming back home to them with joy.

Swap poets for possets to end a meal on a high, rather than feeling down bad. Whatever's got you penning sad songs on your typewriter, find your miracle move-on drug in a batch of salted caramel brownies that can fix you (no really, they can). Find a moment of holiness in a blissful cinnamon swirl, or make a melt-in-the-mouth biscuit that wouldn't look out of place down at the sand lot. If you're dreaming of sweet sixteen, indulge your nostalgia with fluffy, Scandinavian school-inspired buns that'll turn your cheeks pink with delight. Everyone will be looking in your window like deranged weirdos once you've performed culinary alchemy.

How did it end? With nothing but a plate of crumbs.

love
you
ruining
my
li
I
love you
ruining
my
life

THE TORTURED POSSETS DEPARTMENT

Possets were originally an English medicinal drink of milk curdled with alcohol. Fortunately, they evolved into a delicious dessert of lemon-spiked set cream. These tortured possets include a splash of limoncello (feel free to leave it out if making for children or non-drinkers), and are as bittersweet as the cyclone you chose while self-sabotaging. I like to make them in small teacups, but you could also use ramekins or mini mason jars. These are lovely accompanied by something crunchy, like the Lavender haze hearts (page 146).

MAKES 4

Equipment: food processor, 4 tea cups, ramekins or mini mason jars
★ GF

100g caster sugar
Zest of 1 lemon
300ml double cream
A pinch of salt
35ml lemon juice
35ml limoncello (optional)
Candied lemon peel strips, to decorate

1 Put the sugar in a food processor with the lemon zest and blitz until combined. Alternatively, rub the zest into the sugar with your fingers to release the fragrant oils.

2 Put the lemony sugar and cream, along with the salt, in a small saucepan and bring to the boil, stirring to dissolve the sugar. Once boiling, lower the heat to medium and simmer for 2 minutes.

3 Remove from the heat and stir in the lemon juice and limoncello, if using. Divide the mixture between four tea cups, ramekins or mini mason jars. Leave to cool.

4 Once cool, refrigerate for at least 6 hours to set. Once set, decorate with a few strips of candied lemon peel. Serve chilled.

MIRACLE MOVE-ON BROWNIES

Alas, the effects of a miracle drug are only temporary. Don't let that stop you from whipping up a batch of these exquisite salted caramel brownies, though: the mood and energy boost they give you may not be forever, but it should stop you doing anything drastic to cheating husbands. You'll love them, and they won't ruin your life. Eat as they are, or with some vanilla ice cream for dessert. If you want them to last at least a fortnight, they also freeze well.

MAKES 16

Equipment: 20cm (8in) square cake tin (at least 2.5cm/1in tall)
★ GF: use gluten-free flour

For the brownies:
110g butter, plus extra for greasing
100g caster sugar
85g light brown sugar
40g golden syrup
42g honey
225g dark chocolate (at least 70% cocoa solids), broken into pieces
4 eggs
90g plain flour

For the caramel:
80g white caster sugar
55ml double cream
15g unsalted butter, cut into cubes
¼ tsp sea salt

To decorate:
4 tbsp finely chopped pecan nuts

1 Make the caramel first. Put the sugar into a large heavy-based saucepan in an even layer. Heat over a medium-high heat until the edges start to melt. Swirl it around the pan occasionally (don't stir!) until all the sugar has melted and turned golden. Place back over the heat and cook until it is a golden-bronze colour. Watch it like a hawk – it can go from golden to burnt in the blink of a crinkling eye.

2 Quickly take the pan off the heat and whisk in the cream, then the butter and salt, until the butter is melted. Set aside to cool.

3 Preheat the oven to 160°C fan/180°C/350°F/gas 4. Grease the cake tin and line with baking parchment.

4 In another large saucepan, add the butter, both sugars, syrup and honey. Gently heat until it is all melted together, stirring until smooth. Turn off the heat and add the chocolate, stirring until it is all evenly melted in. Whisk the eggs in a small bowl and beat into the chocolate, then finally fold in the flour and stir until smooth. Pour this mixture into the prepared tin.

5 Spoon the caramel evenly over the top of the chocolate mixture, then use a round-bladed knife to lightly swirl it through the brownie batter. Scatter the pecans over the top.

6 Bake for 20 minutes, until the mixture is firm round the edges but still has a slight wobble in the middle, then remove and leave to cool in the tin. When cool, slice into 16 squares.

GUILTY AS CINNAMON SWIRLS

You *are* allowed to cry (tears of joy) when putting the final touches to these decadent cinnamon swirls. Abandon your long-suffering propriety and treat yourself. There's a double whammy of cinnamon, infused into the dough as well as the filling, and a luscious cream cheese frosting to top everything off – we know Taylor herself likes to bake something similar. You should probably write 'Mine' on these (in real life, not only in your mind) so that you get to keep them all to yourself.

MAKES 12

Equipment: traybake tin or oven dish 30 x 25cm (12 x 10in), electric stand mixer fitted with dough hook, electric hand whisk

For the dough:
250ml whole milk
55g butter, plus extra for greasing
1 cinnamon stick
1 egg, beaten
490g strong white flour, plus extra for rolling out the dough
100g caster sugar
1 tsp flaky salt
7g instant yeast

For the filling:
55g soft butter
65g light brown sugar
2 tsp ground cinnamon

For the cream cheese frosting:
55g soft butter
140g icing sugar
100g full-fat cream cheese
½ tsp vanilla paste
A pinch of salt

1 Put the milk, butter and cinnamon stick into a saucepan and bring to the boil, stirring. Once the mixture starts to boil, remove from the heat and leave to cool to room temperature (this is important, otherwise you'll kill the yeast). Once cool, remove the cinnamon stick and beat in the egg.

2 Put the milk mixture into the bowl of a stand mixer fitted with a dough hook, or a large bowl if kneading by hand. Add the flour and sugar, then add the salt and yeast on opposite sides of the bowl. Using the dough hook or your hands, bring together to form a soft dough, then knead for 5–8 minutes, until soft but not sticky.

3 Place the dough back in the bowl, cover with a tea towel and leave to rise until doubled in size – around 1–2 hours.

4 Meanwhile, prepare the filling. Put the soft butter, sugar and cinnamon in a small bowl and mash together with the back of a spoon.

5 Once the dough has risen, put it onto a clean, floured work surface and roll it out to a rectangle approximately 35 x 40cm (14 x 16in), with a thickness of around 1cm (½in). Spread the butter, sugar and cinnamon mixture all over the top of the dough.

6 Starting from the long edge furthest away from you, roll the dough down towards you to encase the filling. Keep rolling until you have a log of dough wrapped around the filling.

continued overleaf

7 Using a sharp, serrated knife, slice the log of dough into twelve pieces.

8 Grease the tin or oven dish with butter. Place the pieces of dough, spiral side up (so you can see the filling) in the tin, leaving a gap of around 3cm (1¼in) between them. Cover with a tea towel and leave to rise for 30 minutes.

9 Preheat the oven to 180°C fan/200°C/400°F/gas 6. Bake the buns for 10 minutes, then lower the temperature to 160°C fan/180°C/350°F/gas 4 and bake for another 10–12 minutes, until they are a light golden brown.

10 While the buns are baking, make the cream cheese frosting. Beat the butter and icing sugar together in a large bowl using an electric hand whisk or stand mixer, until well combined. Add the cream cheese, vanilla and salt and whisk to mix thoroughly.

11 Remove the buns from the oven and leave to cool completely before spreading with the frosting.

mine

SANDCASTLES HE DESTROYS ALFAJORES

If your boy only breaks his favourite toys, give him these instead. Alfajores are deliciously light biscuits from Spain and Latin America that get their unique texture from cornflour. They're as crumbly as a sandcastle and usually sandwich a slick of dulce de leche, but I've given these a Belgian twist in a nod to my adopted homeland and used speculoos (Biscoff) spread instead. I've also coated them in chocolate sprinkles instead of the usual coconut – chocolate sprinkles on toast are a common breakfast in Belgium and the Netherlands.

MAKES AROUND 15

Equipment: electric stand mixer or electric hand whisk, a castle-shaped cookie cutter (I got mine from Amazon)

165g soft butter
100g golden caster sugar
Zest of 1 orange
2 egg yolks
1 tsp vanilla extract
2 tbsp milk or water
140g plain flour, plus extra for rolling the dough
185g cornflour
1½ tsp baking powder
4 tbsp chocolate sprinkles
400g jar speculoos spread (the crunchy variety, if possible – I use Biscoff)
Icing sugar, for dusting

1. Put the butter and sugar in the bowl of an electric stand mixer, or a large bowl. Beat using the mixer, or an electric whisk, until thick and pale – around 3–5 minutes. Add the orange zest, egg yolks, vanilla and milk or water, and beat again to combine. Then add the flour, cornflour and baking powder, and mix slowly. It should come together into a soft, crumbly dough. Add a little more milk or water if it still seems too dry.
2. Bring the dough together into a flat disc, wrap in cling film and chill in the fridge for 1 hour.
3. Preheat the oven to 160°C fan/180°C/350°F/gas 4. Line two baking trays with baking parchment or non-stick liners.
4. Roll the cookie dough out on a floured work surface to around 1cm (½in) thick – alfajores are thicker than normal cookies. Use your cookie cutter to cut castle shapes out of the dough, then place on the lined baking trays. Roll out any offcuts and cut more shapes, repeating until all the dough is used up.
5. Bake for 15 minutes. They won't brown as much as normal cookies, but they should firm up. Remove to a wire rack and leave to cool completely.
6. Put the chocolate sprinkles in a small bowl. Take one cookie and spread it thickly with the speculoos spread – a layer around 1cm (½in) thick. Do this carefully, as the cookies crumble very easily. Sandwich another cookie on top. Roll the sides of the sandwiched cookies in the chocolate sprinkles, so they stick to the speculoos. Place on a plate and repeat with the remaining cookies. Dust with icing sugar, and serve.

SO HIGH SCHOOL BUNS

Skoleboller, or 'school buns', are a Norwegian treat. They're made from a cardamom-scented enriched dough, encasing a quivering pool of custard and decorated with desiccated coconut. Every bakery in Norway sells them, and even if you're too old for school, they're still a lovely way to brighten your day. Here I've gone full throttle and made them as sweet as 16, with a little nod to high school romance in the decoration. They'll be gone in the blink of a crinkling eye.

MAKES 9

Equipment: electric stand mixer fitted with dough hook, electric hand whisk

For the dough:
250ml whole milk
55g butter, plus extra for greasing
1 egg, beaten
510g strong white flour, plus extra for rolling out the dough
12 cardamom pods, seeds removed and crushed to a powder
100g caster sugar
1 tsp flaky salt
7g instant yeast

For the crème pâtissière:
2 egg yolks
50g golden caster sugar
½ tsp vanilla paste
17g cornflour
200ml whole milk

For baking/decoration:
1 egg, beaten
2 tbsp apricot jam
40g desiccated coconut
50g red fondant icing
Liquorice laces

1. Put the milk and butter into a saucepan and bring to the boil, stirring. Once the mixture starts to boil, remove from the heat and leave to cool to room temperature (this is important, otherwise you'll kill the yeast). Beat in the egg.
2. Put the milk mixture in the bowl of a stand mixer fitted with a dough hook, or a large bowl. Add the flour, cardamom and sugar, then add the salt and yeast on opposite sides of the bowl. Using the dough hook or your hands, bring together to form a soft dough, then knead for 5–8 minutes, until soft but not sticky.
3. Place the dough back in the bowl, cover with a tea towel and leave to rise until doubled in size – around 1–2 hours.
4. Make the crème pâtissière. Put the egg yolks, sugar, vanilla and cornflour in a small saucepan and whisk well. Add the milk, whisking as you go, then bring the mixture slowly to the boil, whisking constantly. Cook over a medium heat, whisking, until the mixture thickens so you can see the indentations made by the whisk – this will take 5–10 minutes. Don't heat it too high, or it will scramble. Once thick, pour the mixture into a bowl and cover with cling film. Set aside to cool.
5. When the dough has risen, divide it into 9 equal balls. Line two large baking trays with baking parchment or non-stick liners. Place the balls on the trays, at least 10cm (4in) apart. Cover with a tea towel and leave to rise for 45 minutes.
6. Preheat the oven to 220°C fan/240°C/475°F/gas 9.

7 Make an indentation in the middle of each bun – I use the bottom of a glass spice jar for this; you want the indentation big enough so that there's a border of around 1–2cm (½–¾in) dough all around it.

8 Spoon the crème pâtissière into the indentations, smoothing the top gently as you go.

9 Brush the dough with beaten egg. Bake the buns for 10–12 minutes, until golden brown around the edges. Leave to cool completely.

10 Make the glaze: put the apricot jam and 1 tablespoon of water into a small saucepan and heat gently, stirring, until the mixture bubbles and becomes thick and syrupy. Turn off the heat.

11 Once the buns are cool, brush the dough with the apricot mixture and roll the doughy part of the buns in the desiccated coconut, so it sticks to the glaze.

12 Roll your red fondant out as thinly as possible. Cut 18 small hearts out of it using a sharp pointed knife, then place in each custard circle (as 'eyes'). Slice the liquorice laces into short strips, then place under the hearts to form a smiling mouth.

MENU IDEAS

'I'm feeling 22' kitchen disco:

i'm a mirabelle 116

Bejeweled cookies 150

I knew you were truffles 42

'Like we were in Paris' French-inspired feast:

Long live blueberry and almond couronne 35

Gold rush financiers 131

illicit éclairs 104

epiphany cake 111

'Never grow up' baby shower:

Coffee at midnight cake 54

The (Emperor's) mess that you wanted 80

'King of my heart' engagement or wedding party:

Love story cake 20

Lavender haze hearts 146

So high school buns 162

A pastry shaped like a gown 30

Burnt toast Sunday brunch:

Georgia stars peach cobbler 13

Breakfast at midnight flapjacks 44

(tear)Drop scones 10

Long live blueberry and almond couronne 35

'Now I love high tea' British afternoon tea party:

Throwin' rock cakes 23

Chess game Battenberg cake 32

'Fly me all around the world':

I dim sum-thing bad 84

Snake cake 72

evermoorish lemon cake 123

Miss Americana and the Heartbreak Linzertortes 101

Not-so-cruel summer pool party (pool optional):

Cruel summer pudding 92

Cherry lips cupcakes 64

Snow on the beach coconut passionfruit layer cake 143

key lime green pie 107

'I act like it's my birthday, every day' children's birthday party:

ME! rainbow layer cake 88

Foxes in boxes cookies 61

Donut blame me 75

'Back to December' Christmas party:

Christmas tree farm cake 94

'tis the damson season 122

Grey November Thanksgiving feast:

Call it what you wontons 79

Pecans into place 51

pear and apple brown betty 110

Pumpkin patch cupcakes 26

New Septembers autumn celebration:

Holy grounds maple latte cupcakes 48

Guilty as cinnamon swirls 157

(rose)Mary's song (oh pie pie pie) 15

'Convention of the Tortured Poets Department' book club meeting:

The Tortured Possets Department 154

It's nice to have a friand 97

long story shortbread 120

'It felt like freedom' gluten-free feast:

You belong with Brie 24

A pastry shaped like a gown 30

Wildest creams 56

(milk)Shake it off panna cotta 69

'Take me to the lakes' cottagecore celebration:

ivy cake 124

(rose)Mary's song (oh pie pie pie) 15

Pumpkin patch cupcakes 26

key lime green pie 107

Easter eggs only vegan feast:

Georgia stars peach cobbler (with vegan alterations) 13

Burnt toast sundae (with vegan alterations) 58

Cruel summer pudding 92

pear and apple brown betty (with vegan alterations) 110

Lavender haze hearts (with vegan alterations) 146

© Stijn Van Kerkhove

About the author:

Elly McCausland is an award-winning food writer, academic and lifelong Swiftie. She teaches a Masters course on Taylor Swift and English Literature at Ghent University, Belgium, and has published several books on Swift's lyrics and impact. This is her second cookbook.

Acknowledgements

Thank you to all my volunteer recipe testers for your contributions to the goal of baked-good perfection. Thank you, too, to my friends and neighbours, who risked multiple sugar comas by being willing (and perhaps unwilling) tasters during the summer of 2024.

Thank you to Anna for brainstorming recipe titles and awful puns with me, and for being a baking inspiration!

Thank you, Mum, for working tirelessly to help me test these recipes and being instrumental in fashioning Christmas trees and pumpkins out of fondant. Your cake-crafting talent has been an inspiration to me from a young age, ever since those heady days of giant snails, Tamagotchis and Egyptian pyramids. I will say that you were wrong about the amount of glitter, though: more is more.

Thank you to Alice for your incredible work in styling these bakes; to Ellis for bringing my vision to life (sans Plastic Tomato, alas); to Max for the amazing props; and to Nikki for your enthusiasm and skill in translating all this onto the page. You were all a joy to work with!

Thank you to Marianne and Morgan, and the team at Square Peg, for your early faith in, and tireless work on, this book. It's been an absolute pleasure.

Thank you to Charlie for helping to get this project, and many others, off the ground.

Index

1 3 5 7 9 10 8 6 4 2

Square Peg, an imprint of Vintage, is part of the Penguin Random House group of companies

Vintage, Penguin Random House UK, One Embassy Gardens, 8 Viaduct Gardens, London SW11 7BW

penguin.co.uk/vintage
global.penguinrandomhouse.com

First published by Square Peg in 2025

Designer: Nikki Ellis
Photographer: Ellis Parrinder
Food Stylist: Alice Hughes
Prop Stylist: Max Robinson
Illustrations: Emmy Lupin Studio

Printed and bound by in China
by C&C Offset Printing Co., Ltd.

The authorised representative in the EEA is Penguin Random House Ireland, Morrison Chambers, 32 Nassau Street, Dublin D02 YH68

A CIP catalogue record for this book is available from the British Library

ISBN 9781529956146

Penguin Random House is committed to a sustainable future for our business, our readers and our planet. This book is made from Forest Stewardship Council® certified paper.